Waldo Wisdom

*Small Town Lessons
in a Big Town World*

By Ben Campen

Dedicated to my parents, John, Sr. and Sylvia Campen, whose wisdom and love were the inspiration for this book, and,

To my children, Ashley Campen Carroll and her husband, Andy, and my son, Ben Campen, Jr. and his wife, Robin, all who give me unconditional love and have taught me how to live life more fully, and,

To my grandchildren, Maddy, Jacob, Carson and Kate who inspire me to live life with enthusiasm!

Table of Contents

Introduction 6

Section 1: A Boy's Life in Waldo 9

What is it about Waldo? 11

The Chain Gang 15

The Elegance of Frugality 23

The Accomplished Scout 27

Playing Cards with Dad 33

One Boy's A Boy 39

Making the Best of It! 43

Reap What You Sow 47

You Can Do More Than You Think 57

What Kind of Person Do You Want To Be? 63

The Sky's the Limit! 67

The Early Bird Gets the...Football?! 71

Gaining While Losing 77

For the Love of Football 83

Be Happy, or Be Gone! 89

Hot Summer in the Fields 93

Section 2: Putting Waldo Wisdom Into Practice . 97

When We Are Challenged 99

The Risk and the Reward 105

Finding Another Path 111

Judging Others 117

Win-Win 121

The "Biggest Day" of My Life 127

Was the Glitter Really Gold? 131

Section 3 – The Entrepreneur **135**

Appearance..137

Listening..143

Holding On Too Long....................................147

Norman 151

Duck and Cover 155

The Difference Between Impossible and I'm Possible. 161

The Cat's in the Cradle 165

Love and Respect 169

Forgiveness..175

Knock and the Door Will Open 181

Doing Good in the World 185

Resolving to Make Deposits 193

Relinquishing the Reins 197

The Best Present...203

Introduction
by *Ashley Campen Carroll and Ben Campen, Jr.*

In 1948, our grandparents moved to Waldo, a small town in rural Florida. Our Dad along with his sister, Sylvia, and his two brothers, Jim and John, grew up poor in money but abundant with love.

Growing up in Waldo, Dad gained a certain kind of wisdom that we call Waldo Wisdom. It incorporates small town values, love for your fellow man, hard work, and just plain good ole common sense.

Waldo Wisdom brought Dad a long way. He started his business career with less than $500 to his name and built highly successful businesses in Florida, Georgia and North Carolina.

Because Dad instilled this Waldo Wisdom into us, he felt comfortable in turning the day-to-day management of his businesses to us, leaving him time to do what he loves: writing, helping others and spending time with his grandchildren.

Dad's success has allowed him to do philanthropic work at various places throughout the world and he's received several commendations including the Service Above Self Award from Rotary International, Big Impact Award from Big Brothers/Big Sisters and was inducted into the 4-H Hall of Fame.

Today, Dad writes a weekly blog called Waldo Wisdom with the hope of passing this wisdom on to others. These blogs are personal stories that can help people find themselves and the happiness and success that lies within.

This book is a compilation of those blog posts highlighting how Waldo Wisdom shaped Dad's life and made him who he is today.

We are so happy that he has put his life experiences on paper. The messages in this book will resonate through the generations of our family, and we hope that you and your family will find it as inspirational as we do!

Section 1: A Boy's Life in Waldo

Mother, Ben, Sylvia, Dad and Jim in Ft. Lauderdale before the move to Waldo, FL.

Waldo Wisdom #1

Every bad experience contains a nugget of wisdom if you are willing to look for it.

What is it about Waldo?

In 1948, my parents bought 40 acres in Waldo, FL where they opened a truck stop on Hwy 301 and raised their family. Of all the places in the world, why did they pick Waldo?

This question is compounded by the fact that my family's roots are deep in rural North Carolina. We are talking Revolutionary War deep. But, in 1945, the doctors recommended that my parents move somewhere near the ocean due to my father's chronic asthmatic bronchitis. With my father's health in mind, my parents packed up and moved to Ft. Lauderdale in South Florida.

But as time went on, my parents questioned this move. My father was a traveling salesman, and between his absences and the negative influences of the area, they were concerned about the safety and wellbeing of their children. Also, my parents were small-town folks with small town values. And this 'big city' did not fit who they were nor was Ft. Lauderdale the environment they wanted my siblings and me to be raised in.

One day, as my father was contemplating this dilemma, he passed through Waldo on his way to Jacksonville and saw a "For Sale" sign on 40 acres. This acreage fronted on U.S. Highway 301 and also had a small log cabin on it. As he looked around Waldo, he saw a town on a major artery connecting Jacksonville to Tampa, and he thought, "What a perfect place to build a truck stop!"

As he evaluated the town, he saw the things that a growing family would need: grocery stores, a hardware store, a dry goods/clothing store, a drugstore, a doctor's office, K-12 education and various churches.

But, in my father's infinite wisdom, he saw something that was even more important. He saw a community. Together, my parents decided that this would be a great place to live and raise their four children!

So, our family said "ado" to Ft. Lauderdale without any protest. Shortly after we moved into the log cabin, construction on the truck stop began in earnest. Once completed, the truck stop became our home. Our bedrooms were connected to the restaurant, so we did our homework on the restaurant tables.

This move and business/family plan may seem a bit crazy. But think about the wisdom of their decision. Our father didn't travel anymore, so he was there to guide our path every day. We not only got to see how business worked, but we participated by pumping gas, waiting on tables, cleaning the truck stop as well as clearing the 40 acres. This education was probably the most important of my life.

Indeed, being raised in this small town environment made a lasting and very beneficial impression on me. I was raised by wise parents and influenced by other elders in the community, many who were parents of my friends. Others were the excellent teachers, coaches, Scout leaders and my 4-H leader that became a mentor and close friend.

Thru it all, I gained a lot of what I call "Waldo Wisdom." Over the years, I've continued to gain Waldo Wisdom regardless of where I lived - because this kind of wisdom transcends a locale and is a mindset. Webster defines wisdom as the knowledge of what is true or right coupled with just judgment as to action; sagacity, discernment, or insight. Waldo Wisdom takes this a step further by adding in small town values, love for your fellow man, hard work and just plain, good ole common sense.

Every bad experience and every good experience contains a nugget of wisdom if you are willing to look for it. And you can find it anywhere.... even in Waldo.

Waldo Wisdom #2

The best way to stay out of a chain gang is never to get into one.

The Chain Gang

Growing up in the 50's and 60's in rural North Florida, I saw things that you wouldn't see today. One common sight on Hwy 301 in front of our restaurant was the chain gang. These were prisoners whose legs were chained closely together with each other cutting grass along the roadside. Being chained closely together pretty much eliminated the possibility of escape. But even so, there was always a guard nearby armed with a double barrel shotgun, and of course, those menacing reflective sunglasses.

Back in those days, the government didn't use power mowers or any mechanical equipment to take care of the roadsides. Instead, prisoners used sling blades. The prisoners would swing the tool back and forth cutting the grass and weeds as they walked along the shoulder of the road.

From our restaurant, I usually heard the chain gang coming down the road as they would often sing a tune, usually religious, and I would run out to the front driveway so that I could see them better.

As a child, I was mesmerized by it all. Why do these men have to do such grueling work? Who were they? Why didn't they just run off like they do in the movies?

My dad noticed my curiosity in the chain gang and asked me an important question.

"Do you know how to get out of a chain gang?" he asked. Of course, as a small boy with a big imagination, I thought he was going to tell me a foolproof way to make a big escape!

When I shook my head and answered "No" - awaiting his brilliant escape technique - he replied, "Never get in one."

This piece of Waldo Wisdom had a meaning beyond the moral lesson - don't do anything criminal, and you won't be in a chain gang.

My father was also telling me not to drag around emotional chains like old resentments, hurt feelings, guilt, and regret.

I've often thought about the chain gang when I've seen others forge the chains of discontent. Working a hated job, saying in a toxic relationship, overeating or eating unhealthy things - these are examples of chains that aren't forced upon you – they are chains forged by your decisions. You took them, wrapped them around yourself and joined the chain gang.

Break the chains by loving yourself enough to make new, positive choices. Eating healthy, exercising, removing yourself from unhealthy situations, and treating yourself with love and respect are all positive ways to free yourself from the chain gang.

Regardless of how you "locked yourself up in these chains" (thank you Winston Phillips) and whether these chains were forced on you or not, you can break free. It is your choice.

Jim, Dad, Ben and Sylvia.

Waldo Wisdom #3

The experiences you have tomorrow are largely dependent on the decisions you make today.

The Ultimate Desired Result

When I was a boy, the first game I learned to play was checkers. It was the only board game that I remember we had in our house. My Dad did not allow us to have a TV, but we did have checkers to help keep us occupied when there was free time. My Dad knew that the game of checkers could help us develop decision-making skills and strategic thinking, so he encouraged us to play.

To master the game, one needed to figure out where each move would ultimately lead. You had to visualize your objective while making offensive moves and also formulating a defensive plan to block your opponent from jumping all of your checkers.

My Dad loved to play checkers, and he was quite good at it. I often saw him playing various friends who'd drop by for a few games of checkers. During my formative years, I played many a game with Dad, my siblings, and friends. Playing my Dad was often instructional as he would stop and show me what a different move would have meant. As I grew older, he gave me less instruction, and I learned my lessons through the outcome of my decisions. It was always an exciting, challenging and growing experience.

As we played, Dad would remind me that "life is like a game of checkers: the experiences you have tomorrow are largely dependent on the decisions you make today." That was such a determining piece of Waldo Wisdom as, over the years, I have experienced the truth of that statement. What we think, say or do today will greatly determine how our life will turn out tomorrow.

If we approach the game of checkers haphazardly, just moving a checker to move a checker, we are turning the outcome of the game over to the chance. Life is the same way. When we sit back and let someone else make the decisions for our future, we are turning over our ability to make decisions and ultimately where we go in life.

But even before you start the game, it's always best to know your ultimate desired result. Do you want an abundance of money? Do you want a family? Do you want a particular occupation?

For example, if you want to be a great artist, would you sit back and just admire paintings on the internet? Or would you paint every day, visit art galleries and talk to accomplished artists? The ability to be something does not come just from an idea or a dream; it emerges from the effort you put into making the dream a reality.

Once you realize your ultimate desired result, every move you make - or don't make - impacts your ability to fulfill this desire. Like the game of checkers, adjustments may be needed to reach your goals. But through the twists and turns, keep your dream at the forefront. When you put your effort and energy into attaining your ultimate desired result, you will be able to make it to the winning side of the board and say "King Me!"

Mother, Sylvia, John Jr. (in front), Jim and Ben at the gas pumps in front of the family's truck stop in Waldo, FL.

Waldo Wisdom #4

Frugality does not equal scarcity.

The Elegance of Frugality

I grew up in the middle of my family's small restaurant/gas station on Highway 301 a couple of miles north of Waldo, FL. As a young child, there were always new people and experiences to take in and process. Waiting on tables and pumping gas as well as working on our farm was part of my growing-up experience. I did my homework sitting at one of the restaurant's four tables. And from my time working in the restaurant and filling station, I watched humanity come and go. Particularly, the restaurant was an education in frugality.

One day, a couple came into the restaurant, and I could just tell that they had money. They didn't have that dusty look about them that most of the customers and travelers who stopped by our restaurant seemed to have. They wore nice clothes, along with nice shoes and drove a nice car, all which said to me that they had money. And, when they ordered, they chose the most expensive item on the menu – the fried chicken dinner. No hot dog or bologna sandwich for them!

Our restaurant really didn't sell much of the expensive fried chicken. Our customers were typically hard working people who kept a tight grip on their money, and a sandwich or a hamburger was the usual order. When this expensive order came in, my mother - who did the cooking - went to the freezer and found it devoid of chicken!

This could have been a disaster, but with the grocery store just down the road, this really wasn't a major problem. Rather than tell the customers we were out of chicken, Mama and I drove down to the store, bought fresh chicken, cooked it up and all was well.

Even though we always tried to have some chicken on hand, my parents had the wisdom to know that if we kept too much chicken and didn't sell it right away, the chicken could become freezer burned. Every penny was precious, and we had to ensure that nothing went to waste. And even though we made every penny count, this frugality did not mean scarcity. We always have food to eat, clothes to wear, a roof over our heads and an abundance of love.

The lessons of my family's restaurant have made me frugal. But, I don't think of this in a negative way - I'm not talking about Ebenezer Scrooge frugality. I'm talking about elegant frugality. This is a type of frugality that tells you when NOT to spend money. It's having the wisdom to take ego out of the equation and only doing those things that are going to help you obtain your ultimate desired result.

Elegant frugality spans beyond saving money - it's also about how you make use of your time, your spirit and your peace of mind. Elegant frugality can be advantageous when you are conscience of living life-in-the-moment and making good use of your time. Spinning your wheels, participating in "make work," wasting time, wasting emotions on things that don't matter, spending time being stressed or angry are all the antithesis of elegant frugality. And worst of all, they are a negative indulgence.

Perhaps the most significant manifestation of elegant frugality can be in the positive use of your time, your words, your thoughts, and your actions. It's a simpler, more meaningful way to live and a more productive way to reach your goals.

Ben during his scouting years.

Waldo Wisdom #5

As we overcome hardships, we gain confidence.

The Accomplished Scout

In my youth, I was an active member of the Boy Scout Troop 162 in Waldo. We were a rather small troop, but we had a great time going on camping trips and doing projects using the basics you learn in Scouts.

It was thrilling to be a member of such a great organization that subscribed to the Scout Law: a Scout is Trustworthy, Loyal, Helpful, Friendly, Courteous, Kind, Obedient, Cheerful, Thrifty, Brave, Clean, and Reverent. I learned the Scout Oath by heart: On my honor, I will do my best to do my duty to God and my country and to obey the Scout Law; to help other people at all times; to keep myself physically strong, mentally awake, and morally straight. This philosophy lined up with my parent's beliefs and what they wanted to instill in this small town boy.

I was excited about earning my Scout badges. Each one was an accomplishment. But my bigger goals were to become a Patrol Leader, which in turn would help me become an Eagle Scout when I got older. I could earn a needed badge by leading a group of Scouts on an expedition. So I introduced the idea of an all-day bicycle ride from Waldo to Gainesville and back to my Scout Troop. Some the Scouts were enthusiastic about it, so I asked my parents if they would let me lead such a ride.

Back in those days, Waldo Road (State Road 24) was just two lanes with no bike lane. My mother expressed concern about my safety as well as the safety of my fellow Scout buddies. I assured her that I'd be very careful to ride my bike off of the road when a vehicle approached and promised that I would make sure the other Scouts did the same. My Dad looked me directly in the eye and said, "It's OK to go, but don't be calling back home for us to come pick you up. You're gonna have to be totally responsible for yourself. That's what Boy Scouts do." I assured my parents that I would take full responsibility for the trip and that I definitely would not call them for assistance. "There is no need to worry," I said proudly, "I'll take full responsibility; I AM a Boy Scout!"

A few weeks later, I met up with the others of our Troop who were going on the expedition at the Waldo Scout Hut. After a safety briefing, we set out on the 15-mile bike ride to Gainesville. As was planned, when we saw oncoming traffic, we rode our bikes off of the paved road until the cars and trucks passed, then we'd pedal back onto the pavement, which was a much easier surface for peddling!

Soon we were in Gainesville and began touring around town. After a while, we became bored, and we decided we'd split up into two teams and play chase. We were having a grand ole time when all of a sudden, as I was speeding along on my bike and not closely watching where I was going, the front tire on my bike found its way into a pothole adjacent to the railroad tracks. Going over the handlebars was the last thing I remember.

When I regained consciousness, I found myself sitting outside the door of a nearby auto repair shop on 6th Street where my accident occurred. I had a large goose egg on my head, a cut on my forehead and a pretty substantial cut on my left knee.

As I was coming to, the garage men, who had seen the accident and had come to my rescue, began asking me questions to see if I was coherent. When they asked me if I'd like to go to the hospital to get checked out, my immediate response was "No, please no! I'm fine! I can make it home." What was quickly coming to my mind was the assurance I had given my parents that I would take responsibility for my own well-being. There was no way I was going back on that promise!

As I collected myself and got up to walk, I found it difficult to use my left leg. The pain was so excruciating that I couldn't use my left leg to pedal. Exacerbating the problem was that the torn left leg of my jeans was constantly rubbing over the wound on my left knee. Even though the left leg of my jeans was torn, I dared not cut off the pant leg as that would get me into deep trouble with my parents. Torn pants could be mended; cutoff jeans could not! So I rolled up the pant leg over my knee, and I pedaled with one leg the entire 15 miles back to Waldo.

As we pedaled along, we continued to practice the safe riding habit of getting off of the highway when we saw approaching traffic. Having the use of only one leg to pedal made it quite a challenge to get on and off the pavement. It was exhausting, and I vividly remember dreading the maneuver every time I saw a car coming.

Even though it ran through my mind to stop and call my parents to come and rescue me, I knew deep down that I just had to do keep my promise and take care of myself. My pride and integrity were at stake! I had boldly said, "I'll take full responsibility for myself and my well-being." So, I sucked it up and pedaled onward.

As I limped into the house, with my torn jeans and a lump on my head, my Dad said, "It looks like things went a little rough today." I said, "Yes, sir, they did." My Mom gave me a concerned, yet loving look as she cleaned my wounds and mended my jeans. They were concerned, but I felt something different: accomplishment. I made it all the way home on one leg. And I had kept my word.

This outing taught me a valuable lesson in Waldo Wisdom. There are going to be unexpected potholes that come in the pathway of our life. The test is, how do we choose to handle those potholes? We can choose to be a victim, or we can choose to learn from those experiences. Once we take personal responsibility for playing the cards that life deals us, we can move forward to solve or resolve the issue at hand. If we establish in our minds that we can and will accomplish the task at hand, that declaration gives us the power to do just that! As we overcome hardships, we gain tremendous confidence that will help with the next challenge. Embrace every opportunity (potholes and all) that comes your way.   As Thomas Carlyle said, "Nothing builds self-esteem and self-confidence like accomplishment."

Ben, Sylvia, Dad and Jim in front of the family's log cabin at Waldo, FL.

Waldo Wisdom #6

"Only gamble with what you can afford to lose."

Playing Cards with Dad

My Dad was born in 1897 and saw much in his 66 years of life. He was a year old when Teddy Roosevelt charged up Kettle Hill, and he was 20 years old when he joined the Navy as the United States entered World War I. The Great Depression hit in 1929 when he was 32. At 44, he married my mother just months before the United States entered World War II. And at the age of 47, Dad and Mother started a family which ultimately would consist of my sister, two brothers and me.

As a child, I doubt that I appreciated his wealth of knowledge and the vastness of his experiences. Typically in those days, people had children when they were young and did not fully know who they were. But at 44, my Dad knew exactly who he was. And even greater than that, he was wise enough to know that his influence would help shape us kids into the people we would become.

We lived a "no-frills" life because my Dad believed that it was more important to spend time together talking and building a strong family bond than to be glued to what he called the idiot box (TV)!

But on the occasional Saturday night, mother would take us kids to the picture show. Even though this was quite a treat, I would often elect to stay with my Dad. I loved to listen to his stories while we played cards. The card game we played was rummy. Two sets of three and you won. It was quite something to play with Dad, who was an excellent card player. On many occasions, he would play rummy with the salesmen who came to sell us various supplies such as food, gas, novelties, etc., for our family's truck stop. I watched intently as I knew that our family could ill afford for him to lose. I was quite glad when he won, which was more times than not. He had a knack for cards as well as a great mind.

I studied Dad's play, and I started to feel like I was a pretty good card player. Indeed, the more games I won, the more confident I became. And in my young - but delusional - mind, I thought that soon, I would be as good as Dad or maybe even better! One Saturday evening, I learned how truly good I was not.

On this night of playing cards, I was feeling good! I was winning many more games than my Dad, and I felt I had mastered the game! I was feeling my oats and started boasting to Dad how good I was. My Dad's reply was, "If you think you're good, then why don't you and I play for money?" He knew that I had saved some from selling cold drinks at the University of Florida football games. Thinking of this money I'd saved, and calculating how much I could win from my father, my response was, "For sure!"

I went and got my money and brought it to the table. Dad said, "How much do you have there?" I counted it and said, "Eight dollars." He said, "How about we play for a dollar a game then?" I quickly said OK. In the beginning, I was on a roll winning almost every game! Occasionally, I would count my money and Dad would say, "How much do you have there?" I would tell him $14; then $18, then; when I had a total of $24, Dad said, "You've done pretty good there. Why don't we play for eight dollars a game?" Of course, that excited me to no end, and I eagerly agreed. I was now going to be in the money!!

But, three hands later, I was BROKE. All my winnings and all of my original money were GONE. I was heartbroken. How did he beat me? I was winning in the beginning; what happened?!!

Dad looked into my sad face and imparted a valuable lesson in Waldo Wisdom, "Even though you think you're really good at something, never risk losing everything and never put your last dollars on the line; particularly when you are playing someone at their game. I have many years of experience playing cards, and I hustled you."

Through the rest of his life, my Dad had the wisdom to teach us many lessons that would prepare us for the future. These experiences gave my siblings and me a leg up in life. I was 16 when my Dad died. And even though I was devastated at losing him, I was proud that I could stand on my own two feet.

My parenting wasn't the same as my father's, but the foundation was much the same. He taught me that when we overly protect our children and give them too much, we shouldn't be surprised if they to go out into the world unprepared to deal with the challenges of life. The ability to navigate life successfully doesn't come from privilege; it comes from hard work, dedication, and integrity.

On a side note: Dad allowed me to earn my $8 back one dollar a day by filling out a multiplication chart. Eight days later and now, some 50 years later, I know my multiplication tables backward and forward. Thanks, Dad!

Ben outside his Waldo, FL home.

Waldo Wisdom #7

"One boy's a boy; two boys is half a boy,
and three boys ain't no boy at all."

One Boy's A Boy

When I was a teenager, I walked down the road to a neighbor, Farmer Wasdin, who had a pretty good sized farming operation. It was during bean harvesting season, and he had hired a number of people to pick beans, 'grade' them, pack them in hampers, and then load them on a big truck for market. I asked Farmer Wasdin if I could get a job after school helping to pack the hampers and load them on the truck. Fortunately, he needed another farm hand and hired me on the spot. I felt so emboldened by his quick response that I asked him if he would also hire my brothers, Jim and John. Just as quickly, he said; "Campen Ben (he liked to use our last name first, then our given name), one boy's a boy, two boys a half a boy, three boys ain't no boy at all." I looked at him somewhat dumbfounded. As a teenager, it wasn't the straight-on yes or no answer I was expecting! But when I became a businessman, this piece of Waldo Wisdom became clearer.

As a businessman, the truism of those words "one boy's a boy, two boys a half a boy, three boys ain't no boy at all" became more real to me as I hired and assigned various numbers of employees to accomplish specific jobs. This phrase became my internal "law of diminishing returns."

When I feel I need to hire more employees, I ask myself these questions:

- Do I have enough work to justify another employee or can current employees absorb that work?
- Would promoting someone internally and giving them more duties be a better option?
- Am I set up to manage more employees?
- Am I willing to take a "hit" in the short-term (or maybe the long-term) on my profits?
- Do I want to bring in an unknown element that may upset the "apple cart"?
- Would hiring another person give a current employee the subconscious sense that they don't need to be as productive because this new person would be carrying some of the load?

My basic philosophy is to run "lean and mean." It is easier to get things done and keeps my current employees engaged at a high level. And - I imagine you can relate to this as we've all more than likely seen it - a position will expand into the time allotted. So if you have 20 hours of work to be done, a well-meaning employee can expand that into a 40 hour work week with what I call, "make-work." *(Make-work - activity that serves mainly to keep someone busy and is of little value in itself.)* And that "make-work" eventually makes me do work that I don't need to be doing and slows everyone down! When you run lean and mean, you cut away all the "make-work" and get down to doing what needs to get done. And, I believe your employees would much rather work hard at meaningful tasks than slog away at meaningless "make-work."

Even with individual projects, I like a small team that can get the job done efficiently and effectively. Every extra person you bring in will add more time and more work to the process. Think about this: everyone wants his or her mark on a project. They want to participate, and they want to look good for their participation. If you put too many people on a project, you risk your employees "stepping on each other" in negative ways. Too many employees involved in a project can quickly turn into "one boy's a boy, two boys a half a boy, three boys ain't no boy at all."

Farmer Wasdin taught me an important part of Waldo Wisdom: more doesn't necessarily mean better. It could mean less. Farmer Wasdin was no doubt thinking the same thing when hired one Campen instead of three Campens to work in the bean barn.

Family and friends in our Waldo, FL restaurant. Ben is to the right of his Dad, dressed in his Junior Deputy uniform.

Waldo Wisdom #8

Hardships is an opportunity to overcome.

Making the Best of It!

In my early life, I often had to make the best of it. Times were hard, and we were poor. But, even though we were poor in funds, we were rich in so many other ways. We had loving parents, my sister, two brothers and I were tight-knit and supportive, and the wisdom that came from those experiences made my life what it is today.

Much of the "wealth" of my childhood came from wonderful parents who worked from home. They were always there when I left for school and were always there when I got home. You may think how astounding that was - both parents at home - but they had a clear view of our activities because our bedrooms were connected to the small country restaurant that they owned and operated! This proximity meant that both of my parents were there for us when we needed them and that they could keep an eye on us and the business at the same time.

Because the business was my home, I waited on tables and pumped gas from a very young age. I learned early on how to add multiple numbers in my head and how to make change. This ability gave me the opportunity to interact with customers and ultimately - receive tips. Once, I even got a whole dollar, which was really something in 1957 at the age of 10!

Working for tips was an education in itself. Tips boosted my confidence, infused me with interpersonal skills, and provided some all-important spending money. My dad was one not to give any of us kids ANY money for anything. He was of the opinion that he and my mother would provide food, shelter, and clothing. We kids had to come up with our own spending money. If we wanted something bad enough, we would earn it by getting tips in the restaurant, pumping gas, mowing lawns or selling cold drinks at the University of Florida Gator football games.

One Christmas, things were tight financially, and we kids only received a piece of clothing and an apple. We got no toys at all. That bleak Christmas Day, we decided to make the best of it and opened up the restaurant and gas pumps - a novel idea at a time when all businesses closed on Christmas Day.

And, as it would turn out, were incredibly busy the entire day. With all the other places up and down the highway closed, there were hundreds of people traveling along Highway 301 who needed coffee, a quick bite, and gasoline! At day's end, we had made more money than we usually made in a week! Our Christmas was a whole lot jollier, and those folks who stopped at our truck stop got what they needed to help make their Christmas more joyful, too. We had made the best of it and in turn, made the day better for others.

The hardships I experienced as a child provided me with the best lessons of my life. And I think that is because my parents were wise enough never to let hardships seem like something that would last forever. Hardships were to be worked through, learned from and then banked away. We just made the best of it and moved on.

My parents often reminded me that as life unfolds, there will be obstacles. My father often imparted this bit of Waldo Wisdom, "If you let obstacles get the best of you and beat you, you've squandered what the good Lord gave you - the power to overcome adversity. Remember to make the best of every situation. If you have food in the refrigerator, clothes on your back, a roof overhead and a place to sleep you are far better off than most of the people in the world."

When you experience hardship - remember it's not over, unless you give up. Hardship is an opportunity to overcome. When things get tough, go deep down into the core of your being and connect with the power within you. From there, begin again, and make the best of it.

Ben, w/ brothers Jim and John Jr. in front of the family's truck stop in Waldo, FL.

Waldo Wisdom #9

Whatever we sow, will come into being.

Reap What You Sow

My Dad was born in 1897, and he was in his early 30's when the Great Depression hit our country. He had experienced the 'highs' of being a young businessman during the Roaring Twenties' and then experienced the lows of the 30's. Looking back on it, I feel certain that from those experiences came many of his practical teachings for my sister, two brothers and me.

Most of those teachings came through our simple lifestyle. Our family car and pick-up truck had no radio much less an air conditioner. If we started whining about there not being a radio in the car, Dad would say, "If you want some music, then sing to yourself" or another of his favorites, "Want air? Then roll down the windows!" As you can imagine, we never had a TV.

Our home had concrete floors and concrete block walls with no insulation. It consisted of three bedrooms and a small family room that were attached to the small country restaurant that Mom and Dad operated. The family's kitchen was the kitchen for the restaurant, and the restaurant dining room was our family's dining room.

When I was about 11 years old, dad thought that we should become Christmas Tree farmers and he purchased

3,000 cedar seedlings. In Waldo, we all knew that "idle hands are the devil's workshop," so my rambunctious siblings and I were charged with tilling the soil, planting the trees, hand mowing around them, and hand fertilizing each tree over the years of their growth. This exercise was quite time-consuming for active children who would have rather been playing! I remember at the time feeling that Dad was hard on us; taking away play time.

I was 16 years old when my father suddenly died of a heart attack. His death changed things drastically for our family. No longer would it be practical or safe for my mother to operate the restaurant by herself. So, mother closed the restaurant and took a job at a clothing factory. To help make ends meet, I sold drinks at the University of Florida Gator football games and ice cream at the Gator basketball games.

I often think that my father foreshadowed things to come when he had us plant those trees. The first Christmas after his death, the trees I'd planted and tended to as a child were ready to sell. I put up a sign and sold them on the farm and also cut some them and took them into Gainesville consigning them to various grocery stores. Without this financial boon, it would have been a very difficult year.

Even in death, my father was imparting Waldo Wisdom. This experience showed me at an early age that you really do reap what you sow. I'm certain that this experience influenced me to become an entrepreneur.

But "reaping what you sow" can mean many things beyond agriculture. For me, that phrase means that eventually my prior actions will become manifested, whether it be good or bad.

For example: if I am in a bad mood, that negative energy will adversely affect those around me thus I have multiplied that bad energy many times over. And, when we have a bad mood around our children and loved ones, aren't they then learning that it's acceptable to come home and heap a bad mood on their loved ones? And, what if you get angry and are disrespectful to an employee? That action shows your employees that being disrespectful is okay and can eventually reap a culture of discontent in your business.

Conversely, when we are in a good mood and live a life of happiness and respect, those positive feelings multiply and are reaped by everyone you meet. And then their good mood influences someone else, and it goes on and on.

In this complicated world, are we sowing seeds of love or hate; appreciation or contempt; forgiveness or resentment; compassion or disdain? For, like the cedar trees that once were but seeds, whatever we sow will come into being.

Ben, the young entrepreneur at P.K. Yonge school.

Waldo Wisdom #10

Don't be concerned with what people might think; in reality, they probably aren't thinking about you at all.

What Will They Think?

Upon entering the 7th grade, I started attending school at P.K. Yonge in Gainesville. The dream my parents had for us to attend a small town school all the way through high school had shattered when the County's School Board decided to consolidate Waldo's high school with Gainesville's high school. The consolidation caused a significant amount of overcrowding in the classes which concerned my mother. Mother had heard about P.K. Yonge, which is a developmental research school affiliated with the University of Florida, and that they looked for students from all walks of life and all regions of our county. She eventually was able to get all four of us into this school that she felt would give us the best opportunities for a good education.

My first days at P.K. were interesting, to say the least. I, a country boy, was now in a school with kids from very diverse backgrounds: University professor's children, doctor's and lawyer's children as well as kids like myself. It was also the first time I attended a school that I didn't know anyone in my grade. The only two people I knew at

P.K. were my sister, Sylvia and my older brother, Jim. But, before long, I made friends with children from all walks and backgrounds.

Only a few days after beginning P.K., I went to my locker to get a 5 cent candy bar that I had brought as a mid-morning snack. As I pulled the candy bar out of my lunch bag, one of my classmates asked me if I had another one that he could buy. I told him that this was the only one I had. He immediately said, "I'll give you a dime for it!" As I sold him my candy bar, another classmate approached, saw what was going on, and asked me if I had another candy bar he could buy for a dime. I told him that I didn't have an extra one today but that I would bring him one tomorrow.

That evening, I told my parents the candy bar story and asked if I could buy two of the 5 cent candy bars from the restaurant with the dime I made at school. With a smile and a "For sure!" my parents commended me on being so entrepreneurial. The next day, I took the two candy bars, along with my own snack one, and headed to school.

At mid-morning break, I sold the two candy bars to yesterday's customers for a dime each, and was about to begin eating mine when another classmate said, "I'll give you fifteen cents for your candy bar!" Needless to say, selling a nickel candy bar for fifteen cents was quite motivating! So I sold it to him. That day, word spread that I had candy to sell, and I told potential customers, "Tomorrow, I will definitely have more."

That evening, I took my now thirty-five cents and bought seven bars from our restaurant and took them to school the next day. Classmates were lined up in the hallway wanting candy bars, and I was feeling that entrepreneurial spirit! At week three, I was selling 20-25 candy bars a day! For some of my peers, selling candy bars might have been beneath them, but not me! I was rolling in the cash and was lovin' it!

Before long, I was called up to the Principal's office where I reprimanded for selling candy bars. I was told to stop selling them as the students were spending their lunch money buying candy bars instead of purchasing a nutritious lunch. My immediate thought was, "Well, shouldn't that be their decision?" But, I kept my mouth shut because the Principal told me if I didn't stop selling candy bars, I would be expelled from school. Needless to say, I stopped, and my entrepreneurial venture came to an abrupt halt.

Just a few years later, as I entered into my high school years at PK, I was told the Lunchroom Director needed someone to be a lunchroom assistant, which meant that person would clean the lunchroom tables and mop the floor after all the students had completed their lunch. Additionally, that person's job would include taking out the garbage and also taking out the food scraps in big 30 gal pails to the loading dock where a hog farmer would come and haul it all off. For my services, I received school credit (same as a credit earned in Math or Science) AND a free lunch! Others might have scoffed at such an offer thinking it would make them look bad. But, I welcomed the idea and took the position! It was something that I was not going to pass up!

I look back on it now and think how oblivious I was to the social ramifications of selling candy bars and being the lunchroom assistant. Neither was something that many of the other kids would have done because of fear of what it could do to their reputation. But, I didn't worry about what other people thought. All I was interested in was the end game: a free lunch and school credits!

Throughout my life, this piece of Waldo Wisdom has been extremely helpful: don't be concerned with what people might think; in reality, they probably aren't thinking about you at all. Your fears of what others are thinking could just be something you've made up in your own mind. I encourage you to focus on your goals and never let it concern you what others may think. Be bold and live your truth!

4-H Camp in 1961. Ben is in the second row next to last on the right, in the white t-shirt.

Waldo Wisdom #11

You can do more than you think.

You Can Do More Than You Think

In my early years, I was fortunate to have people in my life that believed in me and pushed me to do more. Because they helped me see beyond the limits I'd set for myself, I was able to gain a critical piece of Waldo Wisdom that would influence my life to this day: I can do more than I think.

Back in my early teens in 4-H, I was very fortunate to have A.T. Andrews as my 4-H leader. He was a man who taught by example. I often played softball against him when the adult leaders would take on the teens at 4-H summer camp. We, the young whippersnappers, wanted to show the adults that we were younger and stronger. The adults often got the better of us by playing smarter and taking those calculated risks that come with experience. And, it was Mr. Andrews who used his experience to the most advantage. When he hit a routine single, he invariably turned it into a double or made what appeared to be a double into a triple or a home run! He was tenacious! He did much more than we young whippersnappers thought that an "old man" in his late 30's could ever do! His performance challenged us to play at a higher level.

In my later teen years, while a member of my high school football team, I remembered my lessons from Mr. Andrews. First, you need to know that the year before, my high school football team won only one game. This year, Coach Gutierrez, determined to vastly improve our performance on the playing field, challenged us to train like we hadn't done before physically. At the beginning of the year, he told us, "Many of you will quit this team, and that's OK because we are going to find out who really wants to win this year. We just want the winners on our football team!"

His speech stirred me up. I knew that I was NOT going to be a quitter and that I would do whatever was needed to be a winner!

Little did I know that Coach would work us as hard as he did! One day, at the end of a long, hot afternoon practice, we were, as usual, to run a lap thru the goal posts and meet him at the entrance to the locker room. On this day, he gave us a little pep-talk. "You are doing pretty well, but if you want to win games this year, you need to do more than you think you can." He ended his pep talk by yelling: "I want one more lap thru the goal posts from everyone that's a winner!" Most of us took off running the 400 yards which were all uphill. Along the way, some guys just quit, walked back and turned in their gear. Those of us who completed the lap met Coach again at the entrance to the locker room. He commended those of us who made it and said, "Now, we're going to find out who are the winners - so those of you who REALLY want to win, give me another lap!" Without hesitation, most of us headed back up the hill. After a hard practice, this was physically challenging, and there were moments I thought I might not make it. Thinking of my 4-H leader, I told myself, "I can do more than I think I can, and I will!" And, that was all it took. I completed another lap - hot and tired - but feeling the victory of doing something I initially thought was beyond my abilities.

After this, before each practice and each game, I recited to myself one of my father's favorite poems:

IF

If you think you are beaten, you are.
If you think you dare not, you don't.
If you'd like to win, but think you can't,
It's almost certain you won't.
If you think you'll lose, you've lost.
For out of the world we find
Success begins with a fellow's will.
It's all in the state of mind.
If you think you're outclassed, you are.
You've got to think high to rise.
You've got to be sure of yourself before
You can ever win a prize.
Life's battles don't always go
To the stronger or faster man.
But sooner or later the person who wins
Is the one who thinks he can!
-Anonymous

That season, our hard work and belief in ourselves resulted in only one loss in the regular season.

This piece of Waldo Wisdom, "you can do more than you think" has also helped me through tough times in my business career. At a time when my markets were struggling, I evaluated the problem and concluded that I needed to expand my operation. I needed to go beyond conventional wisdom and do more than I thought possible. I borrowed all the money the banks would loan me and tripled the size of my failing market in Macon. My comptroller figured I was crazy! But I just kept telling myself, "I can do it, and I WILL do it!"

Yes, it took a lot of hard work and long hours, but I kept the faith. Today, my Macon market is highly successful. And not just successful for me, but for our vendors and our customers too.

Much of my success I attribute to those who guided me, encouraged me and coached me to do more. From Coach Mike Gutierrez, I learned to push through the pain and continually challenge myself to do more. From Mr. A.T. Andrews, I learned that hard work, experience, and perseverance will take you wherever you want to go!

A.T. was such a bellwether for me that I sought him out as a young businessman to help me with various business projects. I benefitted greatly from his advice, work ethic, and his integrity. And our friendship remained constant throughout his life. A.T. passed in 2015, and I miss his love, his support, and his guidance.

We can do more than we think is possible. Because "the person who wins is the one who thinks they can."

The family's truck stop on Hwy. 301 just north of Waldo, FL.

Waldo Wisdom #12

In lifting someone up, you lift yourself up, too.

What Kind of Person Do You Want To Be?

When I was nine years old, my parents talked about something I thought we'd never have: a new 1957 Ford Fairlane. The advertising called it, ""A New Kind of Ford for '57.... with the Mark of Tomorrow." I could just imagine it with its futuristic look and that new car smell! After my dad had gone to the dealerships in Gainesville and Starke, he discovered it was just out of our price range. My dad paid cash for everything so getting a loan was out of the question. In looking back on it, I imagine that living through the Great Depression put him on a very conservative path with money.

Only a few days after my dad had got home from the dealerships and broke the bad news to us, a brand new '57 Ford Fairlane came flying into our restaurant parking lot. It was going so fast that dirt and gravel went everywhere when it came to an abrupt stop! The driver ran through the front door, slammed his car keys on the counter along with a big wad of cash and said, "You can have it all, my car and my cash!"

My immediate thought was, 'This is GREAT! The good Lord has provided! We will now have a new car and some cash to boot!"

Then I noticed the man looked ill. In a pained voice, he said, "I'll give you my car, my money and everything I have if you PLEASE, PLEASE get me to a doctor! I feel like I'm going to die!"

Without any hesitation, Mom and Dad jumped into action. They carefully got him into our family car and took him to the local doctor's office which was in Waldo, just a couple miles away.

When Mom and Dad got back, they explained to me that the doctor thought this man had a bad case of food poisoning. The doctor was treating him, and the man would be staying at the motel next door to his office so that the doctor could keep an eye on him.

After what I thought was a respectful moment I asked, "Do we get to keep the car and the money? That man said we could have it!!"

Dad told us that even though the man had stated that we could have it all if we got him to a doctor, we would not be keeping the car or the money. "Ben, sometimes people say things when they are in a bad way that they would not say under normal circumstances," Dad explained. "He was in a lot of pain, and he would have said and done anything at that moment to make it stop."

Dad went on to say, "I'm just not going to be the kind of person who takes advantage of someone who is in a bad place." He continued, "So Ben, what kind of person do you want to be? The kind of person who profits at the expense of someone else's tragedy, or the person who helps people make it through their time of need?" Even though I really wanted us to have that new car, my upbringing kicked in, and I said, "I want to help people."

Over the next couple of days, my parents would often check on this man. After he had recovered from his illness, they brought him back to our restaurant and gave him back his money and the keys to his car. As I saw the look of sheer gratitude of his face and heard the appreciative words that he spoke, something clicked for me. Yes - I had told my Dad what I thought intellectually at the time, and that was - I wanted to help people. But now, I felt it in my heart. I was so happy that we had done the right thing.

That day, I learned who I wanted to be and, in that, I received another piece of Waldo Wisdom. In lifting someone up - you are lifted up, too.

Ben at P.K. Yonge.

Waldo Wisdom #13

We can all create something better.

The Sky's the Limit!

When I was in the 9th grade, I enrolled in a Journalism course. Writing interested me as I had aspirations of being a sportswriter or sports broadcaster (of course after my highly anticipated pro football career!)

After a few weeks of classes of Journalism concepts, our professor, Mr. Ring, gave us a multi-week assignment to write on a topic of our choice. I was very excited and began writing about my favorite subject: sports!

I poured myself into the assignment. It was a bit longer than my teacher had required and I added quite a bit of "flavor" to the piece. After a few weeks, I was quite pleased with it and was anticipating an "A." I thought to myself, "This paper is so good. I'll probably be asked to read it to the class or possibly to the entire school!"

Basking in my masterpiece, I walked into Mr. Ring's office and handed him my voluminous writing. He began reading it, and after the first few paragraphs he looked up at me and asked, "Is this the best you can do?" I immediately and proudly said, "Yes sir, it is."

Without hesitation, he began tearing up the pages while saying, "You have NEVER-EVER done your best; you can always do better!" He pointed upward, loudly exclaiming, "The sky's the limit! And, NEVER forget that!"

I was shocked, perplexed and hurt. I couldn't believe it! Here was a teacher that I respected greatly, that after all my hard work, had torn my masterpiece to shreds! (Keep in mind, in those days, our writing was handwritten, not typed and saved on a computer.)

Although I was devastated at the time, his words "you have never done the best that you possibly can do" has formed a piece of Waldo Wisdom that has guided and inspired me. Humbly, I know that whatever I've done in my life I can always do better; that it is not the best that I can ultimately do.

Teddy Roosevelt once said, "Do the best you can, where you are with what you have." And, I truly believe that. It can be counterproductive to spend copious amounts of time on a project when there are other important projects to be done or a deadline to meet.

In business, I am a believer in the concept of "continue to sharpen the saw." To me that means lifelong learning; reading the latest articles, taking courses and talking to experts in the field. I know that with a sharp and informed mind, I will obtain better results of what I undertake.

And in my personal life, doing better means being "present." It's engaging with my family and friends when we are face to face. It's paying attention to what they are saying verbally as well as their body language. Even if it's only 10 minutes, I do my best to make sure it's quality time. My emails can wait, the newspaper can wait, and definitely, Facebook can wait!! A particular moment with my family and friends and even new acquaintances will only last for a moment; never to be recaptured.

Think deeply about how you can improve on yourself and the things you are trying to accomplish. Indeed, there comes a time that we have to set a plan in motion. But remember that there is always room for improvement. We all can create something better. Maybe we are more present when we are with others; maybe it's putting in the extra time to improve a business initiative, or maybe it's finding the time to do a volunteer project that means something to you.

Always remember this piece of Waldo Wisdom: You can create something better! The sky is the limit!

Florida Field circa 1960.

Waldo Wisdom #14

*The early, persistent and innovative bird gets the worm
– and then some.*

The Early Bird Gets
the...Football?!

When I was 12 years old, my mother took my siblings
and me to *Gator Growl*, a large pep rally held at the
University of Florida's football stadium, on the Friday
evening before the Homecoming game. Before "Growl,"
there was a "Pre-Growl" which highlighted various high
school bands as well as the UF Band, all of which I enjoyed.
Once "pre-Growl" was over, the UF students put on skits
that just didn't appeal to me, and I became fidgety. It was
then that I became aware of teenagers in the stands selling
cold drinks and apparently making some money doing it.

This activity sparked an idea. In my household, if you
wanted something, you had to earn money for it yourself,
and I wanted a new football!! So, I asked mom if I could
sell drinks and she immediately approved. We went to find
the Coke manager to see if I could get the job and he said,
"Sure!" It was a 'no-lose' for the Coke people as the drink
'hawkers' had to purchase the drinks FIRST and then go
out and sell them. Back then drinks were in bottles.
Hawkers had to pay 12 cents per bottle, and we sold them
for 15 cents, making 3 cents per sale. Mother spotted me

the $1.44 for the initial investment and a little bit of money to make change. The required purchase was 12 cold drink bottles which were placed in a small tub with ice to keep them cold along with 12 cups and a bottle opener. And, was that bucket heavy! In addition to the weight, when someone wanted to buy one I had to open the bottle and then pour the drink into one of the cups. Then, what made it even more challenging was when they cut the lights out in the stadium for a skit as I was about to pour the drink into the cup! Even so, I hustled throughout the night and sold 100 drinks and made $3.00! WOW! I was now so much closer to being able to buy that new football.

Before leaving the stadium, I asked the Coke manager if I could sell cold drinks at tomorrow's game. He told me to show up outside of Gate 1 to try and get one of the limited drink seller passes. Sleeping that night was difficult, as I could hardly wait for the next day and the opportunity to earn more money for my new football, which I really, really wanted!

The next day, I got there early before the rest of the hawkers and got a coveted drink seller's pass. I went in, bought a tub of drinks and began hawking drinks. Unlike some hawkers who stopped selling drinks when the game started (they wanted to watch the game) I kept hustling drinks throughout the entire game which impressed the Coke manager. Indeed, with my love of football, I would occasionally look at what was transpiring on the field, but for the most part, I was all about selling drinks so I could make more money! Needless to say, the Coke manager was always on the look-out for me to show up at the games to give me a pass to sell Cokes!

It was hard work, but normally on a good, warm day, I would sell 200+ drinks, making $6 to $7. That was BIG money for this youngster, and I soon made enough to buy that new football!

But, even after buying my football, I kept selling drinks at the games over the ensuing years. A few years later the Coke Company began dispensing drinks already in the cups and placed 24 in wire racks. This change made it much easier, and I could sell them faster! I then began doubling the sales selling 400 to 500 drinks per game and making $12 to $15!!

As time went on, when I was about 16, I saw that the older guys were selling programs at the entrances of the stadium, before the games. I found out they were making on each 5 cents on each program! Upon further investigation, I learned that the average number of programs that one would sell was around 200-300. At 5 cents profit on each, that would mean $10 to $15.....ALL before the game starting. I inquired of the management about selling programs too and was told that I had to be a college student. I didn't take 'no' for an answer and politely informed them that I could, and would, out hustle and outsell any of the college guys, and if he'd give me a try, I would prove it. My persistence paid off. I was allowed to sell programs and not only did I sell my allocation of 300 programs, but I also sold the "unsolds" that some of the guys had returned. I would take those out into the stands and hustle them during the game (which impressed the manager). I usually would sell some 400 to 500 programs. Once all the programs were sold, I would then go to selling cold drinks as before. Additionally, I added selling peanuts and hot dogs. In one hand I carried the Coke tray and the other a box with the hot dogs and peanuts.

This income helped a poor boy from Waldo buy a few niceties and gave me money to take out a special girl on a Saturday night!

I learned this crucial bit of Waldo Wisdom at a young age: not only does the early bird get the worm, but even more than that, the early, persistent and innovative 'bird' gets the football and money to take a date out Saturday night after the game!

Ben (right) back to school after his summer job.

Waldo Wisdom #15

Gaining While Losing

At the beginning of the summer of my 16th year, I was looking for a job. Being a teenager was (and is) an expensive endeavor! Taking girls out on Saturday night cost money, and I had to earn that money myself.
That summer, Mr. Gunter, (all of us kids around Waldo called him "Uncle"- he was actually the uncle of my good friend, Buddy Wasdin) needed help cleaning out his chicken houses. Uncle's rather sizeable chicken farm was close to my home, and Uncle paid well - 75 cents per hour! I knew that this would be hard work but I wanted to earn some money, and I figured it would be steady work for some weeks. I also felt the exercise would be good for me... but little did I know how good.

The Monday after school was out; I reported to Uncle's chicken farm ready to work. Helping to clean the 200' long chicken houses with me were a couple of other young men whose parents had a corn farm nearby. We would take the manure shoveled out of the chicken houses to their farm and then spread it on the fields. My job was to scoop, from wall to wall, all the base wood shaving that were mixed with the fragrant chicken manure onto the farm trailer and then helped unload when we got to the farm. And oh my, what a fragrance! The strong ammonia smell was - and I struggle to find the right word here - but ghastly is putting it mildly! I also endured ammonia burns that came when the manure dust blew back on me as I shoveled.

We all worked very hard alongside Uncle. And even though he was our employer, Uncle was working just as hard as we were. This job was not beneath him. We all worked together in unison as we shoveled. The only down time we had was when we were transporting the manure from the chicken farm to the corn fields. Sitting on top of the trailer full of manure with a few minutes of fresh air was a very welcome reprieve.

At lunchtime, Uncle gave us an hour off but frankly, I just couldn't eat. After I washed my face and hands, I would guzzle down a half gallon of sweet tea and lie down out of pure exhaustion.

In the evenings, after ten hours of having shoveled chicken manure, a shower just didn't seem to get rid of the smell that had embedded itself in my nostrils. It would take a couple of hours of breathing clean air before I even felt like eating dinner. Also, my stomach muscles were so sore from shoveling, and I hardly felt like eating much at all and often did not.

All in all, it took us more than eight weeks to clean all the houses and install new wood shavings. All the stifling heat, hard work and lack of appetite ended up being the ultimate diet plan. Over that summer I lost 40 lbs, developed some muscles and got into great physical shape. At the same time, I grew more than 2 inches in height!

At the end of the summer, I reported to my high school football coach to start "two-a-days." When I walked in on the first day, the coach looked up at me and said, "Who are you? Your voice is familiar, but I don't recognize you." I quizzically looked at this man I'd known for three years and said, "It's me - Ben Campen!" He looked me over and said, "Wow! I thought I knew what position to play you at, but now I'm going to have to change that because you've lost so much weight!"

At the beginning of the summer I was hoping to lose a little weight and put some needed money in my pocket, but I had no idea this challenging job would change life as I had known it. I had started the summer a little pudgy at 5'9" and 210 lbs. I was now 5'11" and weighed 170 lbs. All the "doughiness" was transformed into muscle. Looking back now, I remember the looks on the girl's faces when they saw the new me. This transformation made me more popular at school and most importantly, made me more popular with the ladies. And because I had saved money that summer, I had the pocket change I needed for dates on Saturday night!

My summer of manure shoveling taught me valuable lessons. Most noticeably, it trimmed me up, developed my muscles, and earned me money, and popularity. But intrinsically, it showed me the importance of teamwork and reinforced a good work ethic into the heart of my being.

But my summer also gave me this great piece of Waldo Wisdom: Sometimes, to get what you want, you may need to shovel a little chicken sh*t. You may not want to do it forever, but it can get you where you want to go.

In my business, I want employees who will metaphorically shovel a little chicken sh*t when necessary. From corporate personnel to janitors, I look for employees who believe that no job is beneath them. If they walk into a restroom at my business and find it dirty, knowing the cleaning person won't be there for hours that they would clean it up. It's those people who I know I can count on to get the job done through thick and thin.

Since my early years, I've never thought of any job as being beneath me. Even in the worst jobs, I gained valuable life experiences, earned some needed money and, many times, found stepping stones to something better. As I went through these times, it was quite interesting how doors to brighter opportunities opened up along the way!

If you don't like your job but find you can't yet leave it, for whatever reason, I highly recommend you put on your high-top boots and tackle the job with a smile instead of standing there unhappy and barefoot in a pile of chicken sh*t.

Ben and the 1964 P.K. Yonge football team.

Waldo Wisdom #16

Find a way to make your dreams come true.

For the Love of Football

Growing up in Waldo, I had an affinity with sports ....particularly football. I loved to watch our high school football team play and, as a kid, dreamed of playing for my small hometown team! The fun, the pageantry, and the camaraderie were all mesmerizing to me. I just knew that when I got to high school, I had to be out there on the gridiron playing football for my hometown school! While I was yet in elementary school, the County School Board decided to take the 9th thru 12th grades away from Waldo and consolidate them with the high school in Gainesville, and my hope of playing for my hometown team was quashed. I had wanted to play on a team with my Waldo friends but now found this dream was not to be!
Even so, my hometown friends and I kept playing sandlot football all the while knowing that we wouldn't get to play high school football for Waldo High.

The consolidation of high schools concerned my mother. There was now overcrowding in Gainesville High School, so she enrolled me at P.K. Yonge School in Gainesville, where the size of each class was limited. There, I became interested in the P.K. football team and attended a game or two here and there. And even though my dream of playing football with my friends for Waldo High was gone, I started dreaming a new dream; playing football with my new friends at P.K. Yonge. When I entered the eighth grade, I joined the junior high football team.

At the beginning of my junior year at P.K., my world changed drastically when my Dad died of a massive heart attack and things financially tightened for our family. Mother was unable to operate the truck stop by herself, so she closed it down and took a job in a clothing factory to provide for our family. Unfortunately, her work schedule did not line up with my football practices. Simply put, she could not provide transportation home for me from practices and often she wasn't able to attend my games. This situation meant that I had to find my own transportation to play football.

Because of this, I often found myself hitchhiking the 15 miles home. Many times after practices I wouldn't get home until after 9 or 10 o'clock, and after games, it could be as late as 11:30 pm or midnight. As November closed in and the cold winds blew, it could get quite chilly if not downright cold standing out there on the road hitchhiking! Also, I came to learn that when you stick your thumb out to hitch a ride, there was just no telling who would stop. On more than one occasion, I had to conjure up a quick story as I turned down their offer. When it didn't feel right, I passed on the ride, even though I really, really, really wanted to get home as soon as possible. But Waldo Wisdom reminded me that the best way to get out of something bad is not to get into something bad in the first place.

As an alternative, there was a Greyhound bus that went from Gainesville to Jacksonville that passed right through Waldo. I often didn't have the money to use this mode of transportation and our practices were seldom over in time to catch the bus even if I did have the money. As much as I loved the game, I occasionally entertained the idea of quitting the team because it was so hard to get home after practice. The late games were especially taxing as I stood along the road late at night, cold and hitching for a ride.

But, I loved the game; I loved it immensely. I knew that if I quit, I would miss being on the team and everything that football it meant to me. So, I made the decision to continue.

As luck would have it, I was able to solve my transportation dilemma. Since I worked in the school lunchroom to pay for my lunch, I had the privilege of going to the front of the chow line, thus getting my plate of food served immediately. As football season progressed, one of my classmates sat down beside me and said, "I'll give you 35 cents for your two rolls." I immediately thought, "With that 35 cents I will have enough to cover the cost of the Greyhound bus fare!" So I quickly said "OK!" I continued to sell my lunch rolls through my senior year. This extra 35 cents a day gave me enough money for the bus and also a few bucks that I could periodically send to my sister who was in North Carolina attending college on an extremely limited budget.

At our night games, I soon learned to barter with one of my friends to take me home. If I had a little money, I'd pay for gas. But more often, using my skills as a fast talker, I would line up some girls for us all to hang out with after the games and that usually would garner me a ride home! In my early elementary school years, my dream was to play football with my buddies for the Waldo High School Blue Devils and to have my parents and friends cheering for me along on the sidelines. When that dream was no longer feasible, I modified that dream because I loved the game of football. This love of football taught me a valuable piece of Waldo Wisdom. When your dream gets tackled, get up, dust yourself off, and find another way to make the core of that dream come true.

The heart of my dream was playing high school football. Would I have liked to have played for my hometown school at Waldo with my longtime friends and where my parents could easily watch me play? Very much so! Did I want my Waldo buddies as teammates? For sure. As it turned out, that was not to be, BUT, I did get to play high school football. And, I learned much from playing the sport; teamwork, tenacity, the benefits of hard work and commitment to a cause. The camaraderie that we developed forged a lifelong bond which we still have to this very day.

I'm thankful it all unfolded the way it did as it helped mold me into the person I am today. All for the love of football!

Ben ready to play football for P.K. Yonge.

Waldo Wisdom #17

Be happy, or be gone.

Be Happy, or Be Gone!

When I was in high school at P.K. Yonge, I loved playing football. It was my game! In the fall, I lived, breathed and ate football! But, when my father died, I spent the summer and other 'off-school' times working whatever jobs I could find to help make my way. Before my senior year, my mother remarried, and she let me stay in the Campen homestead on my own. That summer I worked at the W. T. Grant store and had a second job working construction of the new Post Office and Federal Building in Gainesville. After my construction job ended at 3:30, I would make the 30-minute drive back home to Waldo, I'd then shower, put on slacks and make the 30-minute drive back to Gainesville where I would clock in at 5 and work till closing, usually getting home around 10.

Because my mother didn't have money to support my living alone, I needed those jobs to pay bills and have enough money to take my girlfriend to the movies. And when school started in the fall, I decided to give up my beloved football and keep working at W.T. Grant after school and on the weekends. Practices and games just didn't mesh with my work schedule.

The night of our school's first football game, I was able

to get off work and attend the game. It about ate me up watching my friends out there playing the game I loved! Sitting there in the stands, I knew I had to give up my job and get back on the team.

   The next morning, I went to the store manager to give him two-week notice so I could get back to the gridiron. His immediate and succinct reply was, "Go ahead and clock out now." Surprised, I replied, "I'm happy to give you two weeks' notice. I don't want to leave you in the lurch!" He looked at me with a very stern face and said, "Never forget this young man. When someone wants to leave, they need to leave immediately! If you aren't happy somewhere – you need to be gone!" And he was right. It's doubtful that my job would have been very much on my mind because I wanted to be elsewhere. My happy place was the football field, not working at W.T. Grant.

   In my 30 years of owning markets and malls, I've had hundreds of employees, thousands of vendors, along with thousands upon thousands of customers. The wisdom of "Be Happy or Be Gone" is the cornerstone of my business philosophy. I believe that if anyone is unhappy at our facility, they should not be there. Of course, we do our best to see if there is some reasonable way to make the person "be happy," but if that doesn't work, they should "be gone."

   An unhappy employee is a cancer to the culture and a detriment to the productivity of business. Their negative energy eats away at other employees and very likely makes them unhappy too. For certain, you are not doing an unhappy employee any favors by keeping them in your business. If they are unhappy working for you, give them the opportunity to find a place to work that they enjoy and find fulfilling!

And you may not realize this, but you can "fire" an unhappy customer. We do everything we can to make our customers happy, but every once in a while, a customer will come into one of my businesses and is just not happy, and there is no way to make them happy. In particular, if a customer is disruptive or verbally abusive, we will escort them to the door and politely tell them not to return. It is not worth any amount of money to let the poison of a person like that be inside your business.

Be Happy or Be Gone ensures a happy environment for our wonderful employees and customers who are glad to be there!

To take this one step further, the same is true in our daily lives. When difficulty comes my way, I see if I can do something to transform unhappiness into happiness. If I can find a path from difficulty to happiness in a situation, I'm all about it.

But, if there is no happy resolution to the problem, then I, and I alone, need to be responsible enough to make a change. The truth is, the only person who controls my happiness is me. I am the one that can either turn my thoughts to see something differently or remove myself from an unhappy situation. It's the right thing to do and is beneficial to all concerned. Truly, we all can be happier by making the decision to either become happy with where we are or become happy by removing ourselves from an unhappy situation. Happiness is truly a choice.

Ben with an unwelcome visitor on the farm, a 6 ft. diamondback rattlesnake.

Waldo Wisdom #18

*More than likely, you are to blame
for the situation you are in.*

Hot Summer in the Fields

It was a sweltering summer's day just outside of
Waldo when I, along with some friends, showed up at
the Wasdin farm to pick yellow summer squash for
Farmer Wasdin, whose son, Buddy, was one of my
very best friends. Buddy had recruited us, and of
course, we not only wanted to help them get the crop
out of the field, but we were also anxious to make
some summer spending money!

On the first morning, we all showed up at the
appointed time of 7am to begin work.

As we started picking, we all did our share of
complaining about how early we had to get up in
order to be at the farm by 7am. But as the day
progressed, we teenagers saw and felt the wisdom of
an early start. For sure, it was much cooler at 7am
than at high noon!

My friends and I were furnished with bushel sized
wooden hampers, and we made our way down the
rows of squash, carefully picking the right size

squash. Not too big and, for sure, we were to leave the smaller ones so they had time to reach the ideal size that would fetch a better price.

The beginning of the day was somewhat a piece of cake. We were all rested and ready to go. But, as the hours passed and the sun began beaming down on us, the rows that were 600-700 feet long seemed to be a mile long. It was HOT and tedious work. Unfortunately, none of us brought any water to refresh ourselves! As the morning grew older, the hampers of squash became heavier and heavier and we were all running out of gas.

The Wasdin's house and their packing shed was about two miles away from where we were working, so I asked Buddy if there was a water faucet out on this section of property, and found out there wasn't one. He was quite surprised to learn that none of us had brought water along!

Shaking his head at our stupidity, Buddy said, "I'll be taking a load of squash up to the packing shed shortly and I will bring back some water for y'all." That was music to our ears and our throats! Even though we were thirsty, we kept picking squash as we were being paid by the hour. Also, the folks washing and packing the squash were dependent on us to get the squash out of the field and up to them. After all, Farmer Wasdin was paying everybody by the hour and, for sure, we couldn't, nor shouldn't, hold up production just because we didn't have the brain cells between us to bring water.

Before long, we welcomed the sight of Buddy as he drove up in his pick-up truck. He got out of the truck with a glass gallon jar full of that long desired water! He went to the rear of the truck and went to lower the tailgate where he was going to place the gallon jar. Just as the tailgate came down, the jar slipped out of his hands and crashed down on the tailgate breaking into a million pieces. Water went everywhere except into our thirsty mouths! What, just moments before, looked like heaven, was now gone. We were devastated!

We didn't get any water that day until we finished picking and got back to the packing shed. The next day, for sure, every one of us brought a canteen full of water. And we were all much happier as we picked our way down the rows of squash.

I often look back at this experience, particularly when the summer temperatures in my part of Florida reached the high 90s with 90% humidity. Today, when I feel that dreaded heat hit my face, I remember that time back on the Wasdin's farm picking squash and I subconsciously feel a little thirsty. And I cringe at how irresponsible I was in not being prepared on such a hot summer's day. I was a country boy and I knew better!

For certain, there were a couple of lessons I learned from that day. First, I discovered that I did not want to pick squash or work in the fields for the rest of my life. Finding a better way of making a living moved into the forefront of my mind. And second, the experience taught me that I needed to be responsible for myself. By not bringing water, I put myself in a dangerous situation. When I left my house that morning, I did not take responsibility over my own health and wellbeing, so I suffered a hot, grueling day with no water. I could blame someone else for my problem, but playing the blame game wouldn't have been rational nor have helped me from getting overheated.

By taking responsibility for myself, I have gained true freedom. I am the creator of my own experiences, my own happiness and who I am in this world. With no one to blame and no one to hold me back, I feel that I have endless growth possibilities.

And, by just taking responsibility just for myself, I allow others to decide what is best for themselves. By so doing, I respect them to make their own decisions as to what they determine is best for their life, to live their own adventure whatever that may be.

I encourage you to make this day one of adventure and to take responsibility for remembering the water - or not.

Section 2: Putting Waldo Wisdom Into Practice

Waldo Wisdom #19

Challenges WILL change you.

When we are Challenged, we have an Opportunity to Change

When I was 19, I joined the Marine Corps and reported to Parris Island where Marine recruits in the eastern U.S. went through boot camp.

It was late June, in the dead-heat of summer, when the bus arrived at the reception center. We were "greeted" by a Marine Drill Instructor (DI), who told us in a powerful voice, "Get off the bus and put your feet on two yellow shoe silhouettes on the street....NOW!!"

As a group, we were all different shapes and sizes, from several parts of the U.S. and were of various ethnicities. We showed up with varying hairstyles and clothing. We all were different; many I noticed differed greatly from me - a boy from Waldo - and thus, me from them. However, in just a few short hours things would change drastically.

From the yellow shoe silhouettes on the street just outside the bus door, we were marched into the barbershop nearby and there, all of our hair was completely cut off. Next, we were marched over to the quartermaster and issued our Marine clothing, shirts, trousers, boots and all. There we were ordered to put them on and then package up our street clothes which were then shipped home along with any other personal property we may have brought.

Next, we were marched over to the barracks and given a PRT: a physical readiness test. We were lined up in alphabetical order and first told, one by one, to do pull ups - something I hadn't ever been able to do in my life! Needless to say, I was concerned. The guy in front of me could not even do one and was severely chastised by the DI and then sent to a remedial physical training program, called STB for Special Training Battalion.

Not wanting the same fate, I hopped up to the bar, and with the help of extreme adrenalin, I was able to do eight pull-ups. Next were push-ups. I struggled here as well but did enough to keep me out of STB!

Over the next ten weeks of training, we did extensive physical training, learned hand-to-hand combat, attended classes to learn about the military in general and the Marine Corps in specific. We also spent considerable time at the rifle range and taking leadership tests. This training was hard work, but my Waldo upbringing prepared me for the challenge. In every difficult step, I could hear my Dad giving me this piece of Waldo Wisdom, "Without challenge, there is no change!"

And with that, I ate it up. The physical and mental challenges were making me stronger and more confident about who I was becoming. As I progressed physically, I could easily do 25+ pull-ups and 50+ push-ups along with long runs with ease. The more we trained, the more I grew physically, mentally and emotionally. My confidence soared.

My confidence grew even further when the Marine Corps asked me if I would like to go from boot camp to Officer's Candidate School at Quantico, VA. WOW! ME?! A country boy from Waldo - a Marine Officer?! THAT was quite an ego and confidence boost. Officer's Candidate School would require me to sign on for a minimum of four years of active/full-time duty. As it was, I had enlisted in the Reserve program which only required nine months of active duty.

I will admit that I was so flattered that the Marines' hierarchy chose me to become an officer that my first thought was to do it! But, after much thought, I decided against it. Going through boot camp gave me focus and clarity of thought. It helped me tame my flattered ego. And I knew that military life was not for me.

Although my service was short, it did so much for me. After ten weeks of training, I gained 20 pounds of muscle and lost 2 inches in my waist while gaining a shirt size. When I graduated from Parris Island, I could do 25+ pull-ups, 50+ push-ups and run like a deer!

The physical, mental and emotional growth I experienced while in the military has served me well throughout my life - especially when I entered the business world at 20 years old. I was often dealing with people who were 20 to 50 years older than me and was not intimidated. That confidence came from being a Marine.

I believe that as we walk around in this world, we are made up of all the experiences we've had in life. If we don't try things that are challenging - it's very hard to grow. Even if these things aren't ultimately "for you," there is so much to learn on the path.

As it has been said before, when we are challenged, it gives us an opportunity to change.

Ben (far right) learning mechanics in the Marine Corp.

Waldo Wisdom #20

It's okay to take a risk.

The Risk and the Reward

In the summer of '69, my Marine Corps Reserve unit was in Puerto Rico for training at the Roosevelt Roads Base on the eastern side of the island.

One day while on the bus transporting some us from one area of the base to another, I became engaged in a conversation about football with some of my Marine buddies. One thing led to another, and soon I told them just how far I could punt a football. As we were passing by a vacant parking lot I boasted that I could punt a football "from one end of that parking lot to the other!" The distance looked to be about 60 yards, and since I'd punted that distance before, and I was sure I could still do it.

"I bet you can't do that!" one guy said and soon two other guys were chiming in and wanted to bet me that I couldn't punt a football that far. I calculated how far I had kicked a ball before, along with the potential roll on the asphalt, and surmised that it would be a piece of cake. So, I eagerly said, "OK, I'll bet the three of you five dollars each that I can!" We all agreed that just as soon as we got off duty that day, I would check out a football from Special Services and then would show them my talent as a punter.

Just as soon as our duty day ended, I made my way to the barracks to change out of my uniform and into some gym shorts. While doing so, a close friend of mine from my hometown of Waldo came and told me that the word was out about my bet and asked if wanted to take on any more bets. And, I said, "Sure!" as I thought it was a sure thing!

In just a few minutes my friend came back to me and said, "Ben, the whole squadron (of about 150) wants in on the action! Just how much do you want to bet?" After mentally adding up how much money I had, I told him, "Just $100."

Feeling quite confident, I checked out the football, and we all made our way over to the parking lot where the show was to take place. And it looked like the whole squadron of 150 had shown up, which pumped me up even more!

I did my usual stretches, centered myself, and then made a kick. It was a great high spiraling kick - and my heart soared along with the football. Unfortunately, when the football hit the ground and rolled, it was a fair distance short! I was flabbergasted! I couldn't believe that my beautiful kick wasn't enough to send that football to the other end! It wasn't until I stepped the distance off that I realized that the parking lot was 100 yards - not 60. For sure, that parking lot looked smaller from the bus!! I did a couple more kicks but even with the roll couldn't break 70 yards. I conceded and said goodbye to my $100.

I was rather embarrassed at my failure, and I took some ribbing from some of my fellow Marines for some time. I also remember that I got a lot of pats on the back from many of them too. Did I lose the respect of my peers? No. Many of them admired the effort (as well as being impressed with the distance I did kick the ball!). No doubt, I had given it my all.

This experience taught me a couple of things. First, before saying I can do something, I need to be as sure as possible that it's something I can do! It taught me to gather as much information as possible before making a commitment. And trust me, today I do my best to know how long that metaphorical parking lot is before I bet any hard earned money!

And, it also reminded me of a piece of Waldo Wisdom that may seem somewhat contradictory. *It's okay to take a risk.* In today's world, there is a great aversion to taking a risk. I understand it's easier to settle for the status quo, keep your mouth shut and your head down. But where will that get you?   There is a great quote from one of my personal heroes, Theodore Roosevelt that says, *"It is not the critic who counts; not the man who points out how the strong man stumbles, or where the doer of deeds could have done them better. The credit belongs to the man who is actually in the arena, whose face is marred by dust and sweat and blood; who strives valiantly; who errs, who comes short again and again, because there is no effort without error and shortcoming; but who does actually strive to do the deeds; who knows great enthusiasms, the great devotions; who spends himself in a worthy cause; who at the best knows in the end the triumph of high achievement, and who at the worst, if he fails, at least fails while daring greatly, so that his place shall never be with those cold and timid souls who neither know victory nor defeat."*

I know where I want to be - daring to do mighty things! I enjoy challenging myself, even if it means that, from time-to-time, I won't kick that football as far as I'd like to. And for me, the rewards have been worth all the risk.

Ben (far left) after the Marine Corps.

Waldo Wisdom #21

When you meet a roadblock, don't drive into the wall or go over the cliff – just find another path.

Finding Another Path

In April of 1967, I was fresh out of the Marines and anxious to get a job. I had an opportunity to go to work at a local gas station/repair shop in my hometown of Waldo making $100/week. I had been employed there part-time in my teens pumping gas and doing basic car repairs.

But I also got a job offer from my girlfriend's dad at his automobile auction business in Palatka, FL. He would pay me $60/week (take home pay was $47) and provide me with "some sort of car" to drive.

After giving it some thought, I came to the conclusion that I already knew how to pump gas and do basic repairs, but I didn't know much about the auto auction business. My girlfriend's dad was financially successful, and I thought, "There is something to learn here." The auction business sounded exciting, and I needed "some sort of car" to drive. Also, I knew that if I worked for my girlfriend's dad, I would get to be around her more often. So off to the auto auction I went.

The first auto auction I worked blew me away. Watching what happened, the quickness of the transaction and that thousands of dollars changed hands in an instant, really impacted me! I was hooked, even though at the time I didn't realize how much so.

After a few weeks, I had the process figured out. The 'wholesale' car dealers bought cars from dealerships, cleaned them up and then sold them at auction for about $200 to $300 more than they'd paid. I thought, "I believe I can do the same thing and make some extra money!"

The first vehicle I purchased was a dark blue, four-door, Dodge. Using the auto auction's floor plan financing, I paid $850 for it, and it had a book value of $1,100. I was so excited that I was going to make a couple of hundred dollars! At 20 years old, I was a car dealer, just like the big boys and ready to make many times more on the sale of one car than I was making as an auction employee!

Over the next few days, I spent a lot of time detailing the car, and while working on it, our auction floor manager stopped by to see me. As it turned out, this person was, unfortunately, not in my corner. Evidently, since I had gotten the job through my association with the boss's daughter, he just wasn't all that encouraging in my success as a 'wholesale' car dealer. He said to me, "Why did you buy that old car? What did you pay for it?" When I told him I'd paid $850 for it, he replied, "I think that is pretty strong. That car isn't worth that much! I think that you are wasting your time!" But, I felt he wasn't right as I'd done my research and the car was so clean I just knew I'd be making a nice chunk of change on the sale!

But, when auction time came around, this auction floor manager set the opening bid. He started my car at $500! My heart sunk!! Even from my short auction experience, I knew that vehicles didn't sell for much more three hundred dollars over the opening bid. And indeed, this was to be no exception as the bidding stopped at $800.

After completion of the bidding, the floor manager said "I told you so!" and walked off with a smile on his face.

After I had cooled down, I realized my mistake. I should have never told the floor manager how much I had paid for the car! It was as though he wanted me to fail and I had given him the ammunition to help me down that path.

But what was I to do? Confront him? He was the so-called expert, and he'd say I was upset because I lost money. Complain to my girlfriend's dad? Well, that didn't seem like a good idea either.

So I decided, if I couldn't work with the auction floor manager, I'd work around him. It was time to find another path.

The next car I purchased, I went to extensive measures to ensure he didn't know how much I'd paid for the car. As an employee, he had access to the company records and could find out what I'd paid. To keep him in the dark, I paid the dealership from my personal bank account and had our auto auction accountant make the check out to my bank and not to the dealership where I had purchased the car. When I bought my next car for $800, I told the floor manager I'd paid $1,200. He again criticized me for paying "too much" and when he took the car into the auction ring, he set the price low again! This time, he opened the bidding up at $800. When the car sold for $1,100 he again said, "I told you it wouldn't make any money!" But, little did he know that I'd made $300.   From my initial experience, I strongly felt the floor manager wasn't going to be my advocate. Newsflash to my 20-year-old self: not everybody wants you to succeed. But, because I found another path, I made my situation work and did several positive things in the process:

1. It engrained into the core of my being that there is more than one way to skin a cat. When someone tells me "NO!" I resolve to find another path.

2. It gave me the realization that it's better to be friends than to be right. I could have exploded in righteous indignation and "told on him" but he more than likely would have had it in for me from then on. By getting what I wanted in a way that didn't make him look bad – his negativity towards me didn't escalate. Also, I needed this job, and my girlfriend's dad might have considered the floor manager a more valuable employee than me!

3. It also showed me that there is no shame in a peaceful approach to get what I wanted. I didn't have to plow straight through the problem. Often, I could just find another path.

Each day, I do my best to evaluate the challenges in my life and see if there is a way to find another path instead stubbornly trying to plow right through the issue. If I get upset because of unfair treatment, I am the one that suffers.

When approaching the roadblocks in life, don't drive into the wall or over the cliff – just find another path.

Ben (far right) auctioning at the Albany Auto Auction.

Waldo Wisdom #22

It is not wise to judge a man by his overalls.

Judging Others

At the age of 22, I opened my first business, the Albany Auto Auction in Albany, GA. After working for an auto auction company in Florida for a few years, this was my opportunity to pursue my dream of owning my own business, being my own boss, and making real money! I came up poor, and if this worked, my growing family would never know the poverty I'd known.

Before opening, I had traveled countless miles to visit car dealers hoping they would either bring vehicles to the auction and/or buy cars at my auction for their dealerships.

Along the way, some well-intentioned dealers warned me that automobile auctioning was a rough business. They told me to watch out because of the unscrupulous dealers that would "take you to the cleaners if you aren't careful."

With that warning and the fact I was operating on limited funds, I was determined that unscrupulous car dealers would not take me.

At one of the very first auctions I conducted, there was an elderly man, Mr. Pearson, who wore old bib overalls and chewed tobacco. He didn't have 'the look' of a successful dealer and thus, "couldn't have much money." But, he was perusing the late model cars as they came under the auctioneer's gavel. As time went on, I noted that he had bid-off five of the higher priced vehicles! Anxiety overcame me, and negative thoughts started flowing through my brain. What if this man gave me a bad check? How would I afford the potential loss from a large bad check? Would something like this cause me to go out of business?

I quickly made my way to the auction office and spoke with my office manager, Carol. I told her that when Mr. Pearson came in and gave us a check for his purchases, for her to immediately call his bank to ensure he had funds in his account before she gave him the titles. I told her to page me and let me know so I would know whether or not to release the vehicles.

About an hour later I heard my name over the PA system, and I headed to the office. Carol called me over to the side and said, "You told me to page you as soon as Mr. Pearson came in and paid for his cars." Interrupting her, I anxiously said, "You called the bank, right?" "I did not," she replied. As I started to get my dander up, she held up a hand and said, "He paid in cash. He opened the bib of his overalls and had a huge roll of cash. He peeled off $100s like it was an everyday thing."

After a huge wave of relief had flowed over me, I felt a second emotion. Embarrassment. I had made an assumption that this elderly man in old, worn coveralls could never afford those cars!

Over the years, Mr. Pearson bought a number of cars from me and always paid in cash. I made a point to get to know him and found him to be a good businessman and a great person! Whenever I begin to judge someone by the way they look, I remember the piece of Waldo Wisdom I learned from Mr. Pearson: *It is not wise to judge a man by his overalls.*

Despite our best efforts, we have a tendency to judge others; the person who takes too long in the grocery line, that person who cut you off on the street, the child who said something honest but ill-timed – all these little things can set off our judgments.

But how can we be less judgmental?   I find that by my accepting the fact that everyone is different from me (ever so little or large) and should be respected. Accepting them as who they are, just like they are.

By giving the person the respect everyone deserves, I can curb my judgmental tendencies. That person who took too long in line – perhaps they just had a bad day and can't quite concentrate on the task at hand. And for that driver who cut us off on the street – maybe they are in a hurry to attend to an emergency situation. As the old saying goes, "Before you accuse, criticize and abuse, walk a mile in that person's shoes."

I do my best to remember that these people I am judging are a lot like me. They have families, jobs, relationships, happiness and misfortune. As Earl Nightingale said, "When you judge others, you do not define them, you define yourself."

Ben (center) at the Albany Auto Auction.

Waldo Wisdom #23

Not every transaction in life is a negotiation.

Win-Win

As a 22-year-old aspiring businessman, I opened an automobile auction in Albany, GA. This auction was just for licensed automobile dealers, so to drum up business, I visited numerous car dealers in the SW Georgia, North Florida, and Eastern Alabama. My objective was to encourage used car dealers to come to my weekly auction to purchase cars and trucks to sell to the public at their dealerships. Additionally, I called on new car and truck dealers to encourage them to sell their trade-ins at my auction.

The previous two years, I worked for an auto auction company in Palatka, FL where I called on new and used car dealers. This experience taught me that some new car dealers wouldn't sell their trade-ins at auto auctions. Instead, they would sell them to wholesalers. To capitalize on this kind of dealer, I also began operating as a wholesaler and, in doing so; I could make a fair amount of additional money.

So, here I was following my dream of owning my own auto auction company. I now needed to build a rapport with some dealers, who would buy or sell cars at my auctions and also make connections with new car dealers that would sell me their trade-ins wholesale.

On a beautiful autumn day, I stopped at Dawson Ford in Dawson, GA. There I met the owner, T.K. Cobb, a southern gentleman in every respect, who kindly told me he didn't sell cars at auctions - he only sold to wholesalers. So I altered my approach and said I'd be happy to buy the vehicles instead of him coming to the auction and taking his chances under the auction gavel. He said that would be fine and wrote down five vehicles on a piece of notebook paper along with a price he wanted for each.

I went out to the lot, inspected the cars on his list and took them for a test drive. When I looked at his prices for the vehicles, I was pleased. He had priced them fairly, and I could make a nice profit. But from my experience in buying cars in Florida, I felt that I could negotiate an even better price! As I headed back to Mr. Cobb's office, I saw dollar signs!

Mr. Cobb asked, "What do you think about the cars?" I replied, "They all checked out good; and, I'll pay $800 for the one you listed at $875, $1,000 for the one you have listed at $1,100..." and I continued down the list cutting his initial price on each vehicle by $50 to $100.

As soon as I finished telling him what I would give him for his cars, Mr. Cobb said, "Well, I see we aren't going to be able to do any business today." Not quite understanding what just happened, I said, "I really would like to buy them. Can't we negotiate?"

Mr. Cobb looked at me with a stern expression and said, "Ben, I've priced these cars fairly. I don't haggle with anyone about prices. I know what amount I need to get for my cars and that's the price I put on them. It's obvious you don't want to pay me what I want to sell these cars for - so we won't be doing business today."

When he saw the puzzled look on my face, his expression softened, and he then said, "Do you have a few minutes where we can go have a cup of coffee?"

As we walked to the coffee shop, I kept wondering what I did wrong. This is exactly how I'd bought cars before, and I was perplexed that he did not want to negotiate.

"The reason that I wanted to have coffee with you is, I think you're a fine young man," said Mr. Cobb, " and I admire that you are out here trying to make a success of your life. I invited you for coffee because I want to give you some advice on how to manage a fair deal." He looked at me with great sincerity and said, "Not every transaction in life is a negotiation. When you come across a good deal, just take it. You make money; the other person makes money, and everybody wins."

Over the years, I've taken this piece of Waldo Wisdom taught to me by Mr. Cobb and dismissed the common practice that for me to win, someone else needs to lose. And win-win has proven to be good business. For example, Mr. Cobb and I did business for many years because we both had a mutual desire to see each other succeed. He always sold me quality cars at very reasonable prices and we both did well. And, our encounters were always pleasant. There was no feeling of, "Oh no.... I have to deal with Mr. Cobb." It was always, "I need a few more cars for the auction so I'll go see T.K.! I need to make sure to leave some extra time so we can have a cup of coffee!"

I've also learned that as I cultivate a win-win attitude that it flows into all aspects of my life, and I am more blessed and full. I enjoy the discussion and flow of differing ideas, and I don't feel the need to win a disagreement. I do my best to be in the mode of growth and opening myself up to others and their thoughts, without having to be right, and thus, I learn more and more each day. And by being open to the thoughts and ideas of another, it shows respect and builds friendships and goodwill.

One of my favorite writers, Stephen Covey, says it so well as he describes win-win, "Win-win means agreements or solutions are mutually beneficial and satisfying. We both get to eat the pie, and it tastes pretty darn good!"

Ben auctioning on what would be one of the biggest days in his life!

Waldo Wisdom #24

The biggest days are the ones spent with the one's you love.

The "Biggest Day" of My Life

The date was August 31, 1971. When I awoke that morning, I remember thinking, "I am 24 years old. My business is thriving. And today is the biggest day of my life." And it would prove to be, but not in the way I had planned.

In 1971, I owned the Albany Auto Auction and had spent six months on a new promotion to build up my business. I was giving away a new Mark III Lincoln Continental to a lucky car dealer who had bought or sold a car through my business over the past few months. From what I could tell, this promotion had quadrupled my business so far, and now, in this biggest day, I would make more money than the Mark III had cost. Today really was going to be the 'biggest day' of my life.

That morning, I got up early. By the time I was ready to leave the house, my wife, Dixie, who was pregnant with our first child, told me she was having contractions. Remembering that she wasn't due for two weeks, I wasn't overly concerned. I told her that she was probably excited about our biggest day at the auction (like I was), and for her to come out to the auction site when she felt up to it. But not being completely insensitive and irresponsible, I had her best friend Susan on call just in case.

Upon arriving at the auction site, all thoughts of contractions faded away. I saw hundreds of dealers with hundreds of cars ready to be auctioned. The excitement was electric, and I was consumed with all that was taking place on 'the biggest day' of my life!

But life intervened, and only a few hours later, as the auction was moving fast, I was paged to the office. Susan excitedly told me that Dixie had just delivered a baby girl and that I was now a papa! I thought, "A Papa? A PAPA!" At that moment, my focus changed. The excitement of the auction fell away. No longer was the auction important; my only interest was getting to the hospital to see my daughter.

When the elevator door opened on the maternity floor, there was a sign saying "no admission at this time." Ignoring the sign, I made my way down to the nurse's station and told them that I just had to see my little girl. They said if I walked up to the nursery, they would bring her up to the window so I could see her; and they did. I was awe struck! She was healthy and beautiful – and she was my little girl.

Looking at my daughter, I felt a shift in my soul, in my world, in what was important. That day, she taught me a valuable piece of Waldo Wisdom. At 24, the 'biggest day' in my life had nothing to do with an auction or making money. It had everything to do with her.

John Lennon said it best, "Life happens while you are

making other plans." (He must have been from Waldo!) As
Ashley, Ben Jr. and I travel down the road of life together,
all of my biggest days have revolved around them and their
growing families. They are more important to me than
chasing material things. And I am a richer man for it. The
biggest days are truly the ones spent with those you love.

The transport truck that liberated six of Albany Auto Auction's cars.

Waldo Wisdom #25

If you let it, success can come from failure.

Was the Glitter Really Gold?

As I was beginning in my business career, I owned and operated an auto auction business in Albany, GA. I had worked a couple of years in the auto auction business in Palatka, FL and now that I had ventured out on my own, I loved being my own boss. It was now was all up to me to run the business, and its success depended on the decisions I made and the people I employed to assist me in the operations.

I worked hard, long hours. Frankly, that didn't bother me at all. I was young, welcomed the challenges and relished being my own boss.

My auction house was for auto dealers only. At least, that what I advertised it to be. When a new "dealer" came to the auction to do business, we let THEM fill out a registration form, and it was up to THEM to fill out their pertinent information, including their dealer's license number. We just took THEIR word for it, that what they filled out was, indeed, truthful and correct. Remember, this was in the early 70's - way before the Internet and the ability to verify information immediately. Dealers filled out the new dealer form, and we welcomed them as trusted customers to our auction.

After a couple of years of running this business, I felt confident that I knew the business and that I had a gift for accessing situations and people as they entered my business. One auction day, an empty automobile transport truck that could haul six cars entered the auction yard. Following the truck was a brand new Cadillac driven by a very well dressed man carrying an alligator-skin briefcase. I watched with great anticipation as he entered the office and filled out the new Dealer Registration form. Needless to say, I was elated when he soon told me that he had come to purchase six late model cars! Most of my dealers did not dress or look like this, and I was quite impressed by his presence and his apparent wealth.

True to his word, he indeed, did purchase six late model cars. He paid for his cars with bank drafts - a customary method of payment during that era. What that meant was; we kept the titles, put them into the draft envelope and then we would take the drafts to our bank who would send them to the customer's bank. The customer would pay for and then receive that title and then the bank would deposit the funds into my account.

The only problem was; the new dealer never went to the bank to pay the drafts. About ten days later our bank informed us that the drafts had been returned unpaid. We retrieved them from our bank and placed a call to the new dealer at the number he had written on his registration. We found out that the number was a non-working number! Next, we attempted to reach him by mail to no avail.

Eventually, we found out he had taken the cars to the state of Alabama, which at the time was a no-title state where license tag registration determined car ownership, and he registered the cars and bought a tag for each of them. He took the cars to Kansas City, MO and sold them at an auto auction there, where he received payment from the auction company. He received immediate payment as he produced what was then legal title because of the Alabama tag registration.

I never did see or hear from him again, nor did I ever get paid for the cars. At that point in my life, I hadn't learned the entire meaning of the Waldo Wisdom "You can't judge a man by his overalls." I'd learned that a man dressed poorly could be an honest man, but I had yet to learn that a man dressed nicely could be a dishonest man! It was an expensive lesson to learn!

This experience caused me to re-evaluate if I wanted to remain in the auto auction business in Albany, GA or look at pursuing the real estate development and brokerage business back in FL, which, shortly after that, is what I did.

And, it all worked well. At that moment, the real estate market was on the verge of exploding in Florida and everything unfolded in a very positive way. I benefitted from a bad experience because I took a positive action.

My experiences with the well-dressed man afforded me a gem of Waldo Wisdom: Success can come from failure. Instead of letting failure defeat me, I learned from it, redirected my path and navigated around it. If I had let this experience get the better of me, I could have become a suspicious and bitter auto auction owner. I would have been miserable and probably would have run that business into the ground. Making a positive course correction meant a better life for my family and me.

What glittered in the well-dressed buyer was not gold, but the real estate auction business that grew from this experience turned out to be golden!

Section 3 – The Entrepreneur

Ben using his auction skills for charity.

Waldo Wisdom #26

You should not judge a book by its cover,
but others may judge you by yours.

Appearance

When I was in my early 30's, I was driving a very long, very boring, very brown, four-door Buick. It was a good car, but it wasn't me. I had in mind a car with a sportier, yet professional, look. I didn't want just any car; I wanted the car my Dad said was THE best car ever made. That car was a Mercedes Benz. When I was a child, our family couldn't afford one, so we drove a Ford. As my father regaled the qualities of a Mercedes, I told myself that I would own that brand of car one day. And, on that day in my mid 30's, this is what I wanted to buy.

Before I made this bold purchase, I mentioned it to some family members and friends. The consensus was, that driving a Mercedes would appear ostentatious and that it wouldn't be good to be seen driving one at my young age, early in my business life.

Needless to say, that was not what I wanted to hear. But I took the advice of my friends and family and started to look for a car that wouldn't be so ostentatious.

So, I began looking at just about every make and model, trying to find that perfect car that was NOT a Mercedes.

The more I looked, the more I felt that any other car could not fit the bill. None seemed right.

At another friend's suggestion, I read some consumer magazines about automobiles. I thoroughly read the articles and reports regarding resale value as well as maintenance issues and customer satisfaction. I was desperately searching for an answer, and there it all was, in black and white, Mercedes was THE car.

So, I headed out to the Mercedes dealership and the car that immediately caught my eye was a maroon 300D. After the test drive, I knew that this Mercedes was THE car for me!

Now that I'd found the car and had thrown my friends and family's advice to the wind, the issue now was how was I going to pay for this car? I only had about 10% of the cost in my bank account. I called my bank and asked if they would finance the vehicle, but they were not making any car loans at this time but said that they would do a commercial loan on a 90-day note. I pondered over the thought that I had no exact plan of how I was going to pay all of this money back at the end of 90 days. What I did know was, I wanted this car and that I would do whatever it took to pay the bank off - even if it took liquidating personal as well as business assets. Deep down inside, I knew that this car was meant for me! So, I borrowed the entire amount of the cost of the car from the bank. When I picked it up, I was very excited to get my dream car and yet anxious about the loan at the same time. And that is where serendipity walked in.

The day I ordered my new car, I received a call from a gentleman who lived in Leesburg asking me to conduct an auction of some real estate he owned. He said, "Whenever you're down this way, give me a call, and you can stop by and see the property." Since I was picking up my new car in Orlando (only a few miles from Leesburg) the next day, I went ahead and made an appointment to see him on the way back to Gainesville.

When I arrived at Mr. Montgomery's home, I parked directly in front of his front door on the circular drive. He met me at the door and said we should take a look around his place and talk more about my services. After a few minutes of walking the property, I retrieved my briefcase and the portfolio from my new car, which contained previous auction flyers as well as a few letters of recommendation.

As I started to go thru the standard presentation I usually gave to prospective clients; Mr. Montgomery interrupted me saying, "You don't need you to go thru all of that with me. I figure anyone that can drive a new Mercedes knows what he's doing! I'm ready to sign the auction agreement." As it turned out, the new Mercedes wasn't an obstacle after all and, in fact, was a major contributing factor towards getting the job!

When I conducted the auction, it proved to be a huge success! Mr. Montgomery was quite pleased with the price his property brought, and I was elated that my commission more than covered the entire cost of my new Mercedes!

This experience taught me an interesting piece of Waldo Wisdom: Many times in life, appearances count. Personally, I do my best to look past appearances because they may be deceiving. But the outcomes of job interviews, business meetings and even meeting your girlfriend's parents can be influenced by your appearance. When we make an effort, the other person feels respected. And that extra effort is a simple step to help you reach your goals.

Studies show that your appearance also has a bearing on your income level. But interestingly enough, appearance came third to a smile and one's attitude. As I look back on my first meeting with Mr. Montgomery, my new car might not have been the only thing that encouraged him to hire me. No doubt, on that day, my smile was broader than usual, and my attitude was extremely positive as my confidence level was at an all-time high, boosted by driving the car of my dreams.

Your appearance is your brand and can help you get where you want to go. A positive attitude, a happy smile and making an effort with your appearance are always a very good thing!

Ben as a young businessman.

Waldo Wisdom #27

Listening is a sign of respect.

Listening

Have you ever heard someone express an idea that made you react with negativity? Thoughts of, "There's no way I'm doing that!" or "That isn't the way I'd do it!" can flood your thoughts before you hear the idea in its entirety. I've had this experience, and if I'd have given in to that negative reaction, I'd have missed out on a great opportunity.

It was 6:30 am in Gainesville, FL in 1978. I was up and out the door to a restaurant in East Gainesville where a group of 20 to 30 seasoned community movers and shakers gathered to chat about sports, politics as well as business ideas.

As a young businessman myself, I enjoyed being in their midst. I was able to learn from their ideas and experiences and insights.

When I sat down at an open chair at one of the tables, a man I had known only on the periphery, J C – a former county Judge, beckoned me over from an adjacent table. Since I knew he was a real estate investor, I thought he might need my real estate auctioneering services. After some pleasantries, he got down to it and asked, "Would you have any interest in going in on a motel purchase in Atlanta?"

My reaction was immediate, "I appreciate the offer but buying a motel in Atlanta is the last thing I would ever want to do." He started laughing and said, "I've been observing you over the past few years, and I took you to be smarter than that." "What do you mean?" I asked. "You made a decision without listening to the whole story," said JC.

JC was a very prominent person in the community of whom I had the utmost respect. Additionally, I knew JC was smart and successful and that I should hear him out. I humbly said, "You are so right, I wasn't thinking. Tell me about this motel idea."

After some explanation, the deal started to make sense. And, later that morning, I found myself on a plane with JC heading to Atlanta. Once I evaluated the property, had a look at the books and made some projections, I was confident this venture would be successful.

And successful it was. After operating the motel for just a little over a year, a man from India contacted us and bought it, paying us over double of what we had paid for it.

Needless to say, I was very glad the Judge implored me to listen to the whole story and that I chose to hear it! I stretched beyond my personal limits and profited.

What aren't we hearing when people talk to us? The benefits of choosing to listen can be great regardless if you agree with their idea or not. If you allow someone to tell you their thoughts and ideas, they will feel valued that you took the time to hear them. Also, in listening to them thoroughly, you will understand them and their ideas.

After you've listened, you may decide their idea isn't for you, and that's okay. Listening is a true sign of respect. They will know you listened and took their idea seriously.

And don't think this is just a business concept. In our personal lives, and, quite often we may take those closest to us for granted. The truth is, we all want to be heard. I encourage you to listen – deeply listen - to what people say. It is not only a sign of respect but an acknowledgment that they are important to you!

Leo Buscaglia said it best, "Too often we underestimate the power of a touch, a smile, a kind word, a listening ear, an honest compliment, or the smallest act of caring, all of which have the potential to turn a life around."

And who knows? Just by listening, the life you might turn around could be your own.

An actual key from Ben's hotel, the Dinkler Belvedere Motor Inn.

Waldo Wisdom #28

Leave something for the next guy.

Holding On Too Long

Back in the late 70's, former Alachua County Judge John Connell and I purchased a 94-room motel in Atlanta from a real estate investment trust. Due to the motel's very low occupancy rate, they were going to tear down the motel sell the property for its land value. When John learned of this via a contact in Atlanta, he asked me if I'd go in as a 50/50 partner.

After looking over the physical condition of the property, I inquired of the motel manager about their occupancy rate. When the manager told me they averaged renting 16 rooms a day from that 94 room property, I went into problem-solving mode.

I asked the manager if they tried renting rooms out on a weekly or monthly basis, and she said, "That would be disastrous! People who rent by the week or month would wear out the carpet because they will walk the same path to and from the bedroom to the bathroom, and that wouldn't be good." You know that quizzical expression a dog makes as it cocks its head to one side? Well, that was me. Was she seriously saying something that bizarre?

With the motel in good physical condition, it potentially had some good years left, but I needed to check the market to verify my thoughts.

So, I immediately bought a newspaper and began looking in the classifieds (this was well before Internet and Google) to see if there were weekly/monthly rooms listed and see average rental rates. Indeed, there were such rooms, and I noted the rental rates. Using an average rate, I ran the numbers, which proved very positive, shared them with John and we purchased the property.

Since we didn't live in Atlanta, an honest and efficient management team was a must. We were extremely fortunate that John's daughter and a friend of hers were available to operate the motel.

With that important step completed, the next thing I did was to prepare an announcement stating 'The Dinkier Belvedere is now renting rooms by the week and by the month." I then mailed it to area trade schools, colleges, hospitals and construction companies. Because the daily rental rate was higher than the weekly, we reserved 16 rooms to rent by the day, and the remainder would be for our longer occupants.

Within a couple of months, the concept had worked, and the motel was running at full occupancy. This trend continued month after month. We were making good money, and all was well.

Noting our success, a man from India, Mr. Patel, inquired about purchasing the property. Mr. Patel's offer was more than double what we had paid, but I thought we should wait for a higher sales price. The motel was making enough money to warrant a higher price and I thought we should hold out and get all that it was worth.

When I discussed this with John, he laughed and said, "You know, we've been fortunate to have Mary and her friend running the place for us while we continue to live 300 miles away. But, there is no guarantee that they will continue to manage the motel in the future." He went on to say, "Furthermore Ben, remember: always leave something for the next guy." Those words resonated with me as they came from a man whom I very much respected. John was a wise man, and I learned from him a great lesson that day.

What he was saying was not to hold on too long. The motel was having a good run, and it was time sell, book our profits, and celebrate. If the motel continued to succeed, well, you've still made good money, so why worry? You've left something for the next guy.
So we sold it.

With my portion of the sale proceeds, I purchased a farm, and within a year, I made a handsome profit from it as well. That would not have been possible if John and I hadn't sold the motel. And if I'd have waited, the potential was there for the business to slide and with a distinct possibility for a smaller sale price.

Business is about relationships. When you create a win-win situation, you let the business world know that you have integrity and creates other opportunities. I believe that you get what you give - good or bad.

To leave something for the next guy is not only good business, but it's just simply a good thing to do.

One of Norman's signs that is still in use after 30+ years at Smiley's in Fletcher, NC.

Waldo Wisdom #29

Help your customers succeed.

Norman

When I was starting out in the real estate and auction business, I was in need of a sign painter. (Yes - we had to hand paint signs then!) In my line of business, I spent a lot of advertising dollars on signs. So finding a good sign painter was crucial.

As luck would have it, I met an excellent sign painter, Norman Grove. The price he charged was reasonable, and he did a great job. I always admired Norman's attention to detail - such as painting the edges of the boards to help make them weatherproof and always putting ample paint on the boards so that they would have a long lifespan. He was all about giving his customer a quality product.

As part of his service, he delivered the signs to me, driving many miles from his workshop to my office. And, as I developed new businesses throughout the South, I would always use Norman to paint the signs I needed for that venture or occasion. I knew the signs would be done right and at a good price; both of which were important to me as a young businessman.

Every time I needed signs; I called on Norman. He was always very appreciative of the work I sent his way. And I was always grateful to have someone I could truly depend on supplying these needed signs.

After we had worked together for several years, I was budgeting sign costs for a project, and it hit me like a ton of bricks.....Norman had never increased the prices for the signs he made for me. I had clearly seen where the cost for everything else had increased over the years as I reviewed my budget sheet.

The very next time I saw Norman, I told him that he had never raised his prices and that I wanted to pay him more for his excellent work. He quickly said that he wouldn't let me do it. I knew he had pretty much retired and that I was his only remaining customer. "Ben, I enjoy doing work for you because you've always been an excellent customer who does what he says and pays me immediately upon delivery," said Norman. "Painting signs for you gives me something to do. And besides, I feel like I've been a part your journey. I know that signs are an important part of what you do, so I'm going to keep my pricing where it is. I never want there to be any hesitation on your part to order a sign because of the cost."

Needless to say, I kept ordering and ordering signs from him, for any and everything I had going on. Even when I conducted real estate auctions as far away as Texas, I had Norman paint them and then I would truck them there. That's how good he was! Not only as a painter who cared about his product, but as a person who cared about the success of his customer!

Norman passed away a few years ago, and I think of him often with great respect for who he was and what he meant to me and my success.

Even though we've transitioned to more high-tech ways of making signs, there are still many original Norman Grove signs at my markets, and they have weathered the test of time (some now for 30 years that still look great!)

Today, I look at the way he conducted his business, and I marvel at the beauty of it. He had a philosophy of excellence as a sign painter and as a human being. Norman did what he loved, was loyal to a fault, enjoyed and valued his customers, cared deeply about the quality of his product and did what he could to help his customers be successful.

Just think how wonderful the world of business would be if we were all like Norman! And, I believe if we followed his example, we'd all be a little happier, too.

Ben (center) and his daughter, Ashley (far right) in Russia.

Waldo Wisdom #30

We are more alike than you think.

Duck and Cover

In 1951, a film entitled "Duck and Cover" was released and shown to school children all over the United States. Because the Soviet Union detonated their first nuclear device the year before, the U.S. government wanted to prepare the population for a nuclear attack. Thus, the Duck and Cover campaign was born. Communities built bomb shelters; schools performed bomb drills, and the film "Duck and Cover" was shown to all schoolchildren.

And as a young child, I found all of this disconcerting. Who were these people that wanted to hurt us? And there was talk about Soviet spies in America. As an impressionable child, all of the Soviet Union was evil, and all they wanted to do was hurt us.

Fast forward to 1993. David Tyler Scoates, a renowned minister, and close friend called to invite me to travel with him, his wife Vonda and a small group of people on a goodwill trip to Russia. The Soviet Union had been dissolved the year before, and the focus of this trip was to advise and support Russian farmers, helping them to get better production from their crops as well as to extend a hand of friendship.

And of course, I wanted to go! To travel to the former Soviet Union and see my country's former "enemy" was an experience I did not want to miss. I also thought it would be a great trip for my daughter Ashley and me to experience together. Not only would a trip to Russia be exciting and educational for her, but it would also give me a chance to have a special trip with my 21 years old daughter.

One of the things we wanted to do was to take gifts to the children and the adults as well. Luggage space was limited, yet I wanted to give something meaningful to the adults. I read that they liked blue jeans, so off to the store I went, buying various sizes, mostly large or extra-large as that was the size I thought all Russians were!

After being in Moscow a couple of days, our group loaded on the bus and headed to the farm we were sponsoring to meet with the farmers, the clergy, and governmental officials. There, we would do a ceremonial planting of potatoes and then enjoy lunch with all of them. I brought the jeans and promptly put them on the rack above my seat to have them handy to get to once we reached the farm. As it turned out, the ride to the farm took a few hours, and, with all the excitement and the ceremony looming, I forgot about the jeans as I exited the bus.

After the introductions, we each participated in the ceremonial planting of potatoes. Afterward, we made our way to the feast they had prepared for us set on tables under large trees next to a beautiful lake. There were no chairs, so we stood on one side of these long tables and conversed with the locals who were standing on the opposite side. Narrow in width, it made for great conversation, albeit, they were the ones speaking our language, not us speaking theirs! Across from Ashley and myself were a couple of farmers and clergy. At first, they were referring to Ashley as my wife - this happened several times while we were there as older men marrying younger women is common there. Explaining that she was my daughter, they immediately said they want to marry her; quite funny, love at first sight! We all had a good laugh.

One thing that was familiar to me was farm life. A farm is a farm regardless of where you are in the world. There are necessary chores, work schedules to follow, and hard work to be done. And these were good, hard working people.

Once lunch was over, we began saying our goodbyes and boarded the bus. Once aboard, I looked out of the window and saw a couple of the farmers standing there to see us off and was reminded that I hadn't given the jeans away. So, I immediately grabbed them, hopped off the bus and reached out the jeans to hand to the farmers. They both shook their heads 'NO'. I couldn't understand, and I asked our Russian guide to find out why they wouldn't accept my gift. They told her that they couldn't accept my gift as they didn't have a gift to give me in return. I told her to please tell them that their gift to me would be to accept my gift. She translated what I said, and they gratefully accepted the jeans. Then, one of the farmers took his notepad and wrote and handed me a note. I had our guide read it to me; "In appreciation of your generous gift to us, my family and I would like to host you and your wife to dinner at our home tonight." WOW!! That was touching and something that I really wanted to do. But, it wasn't possible, so I thanked him for his kind gesture, and we headed back to Moscow.

On the drive back, I couldn't stop thinking that these two farmers who were about my age. If we'd have gone to war with Russia, they could have been the "enemy" that I was trained to kill when I was in the Marines some 25 years earlier. My childhood perception of the Soviet enemy from whom I had to "duck and cover" was challenged. These were wonderful, hardworking people. From their own volition, they wanted to be my friend, not my enemy.

While in Moscow, Ashley and I visited their one and only flea market. There, we met a young man with a booth who spoke English. While I was interacting with this young man, Ashley, and a girlfriend decided to walk around the market. This vendor was quite pleasant, and we had a very enjoyable conversation. Soon, he invited me to come around to the other side of his table where he asked his wife to hand him something: a bottle of Vodka! He unscrewed the cap and handed it to me and said, "We drink to brotherly love!" We each took a swig and then commenced to drink to world peace. The irony of drinking to world peace with my "enemy" was not lost on me. We continued to drink to happiness, life, and joy as we conversed. We talked about his concerns for the future and his desire for his country to stay in peace.

Once Ashley returned, my new friend said something to his wife and then said to me, "My wife and I would like to have you and your wife to come stay with us for a few days as our guests." I thought, how kind and generous of an invitation, but due to our group's schedule, we had to decline.

As the plane lifted off the Moscow runway a few days later, I couldn't help but think about these wonderful people. They were just like me. And like my family and friends; they want to live their life in freedom and joy. They didn't want to harm me; they wanted to be my friend. And I had the same feelings for them.

I am glad that I was able to have this experience. And it was life altering. It taught me that in a world filled with conflict, people are living in war zones who are just like you and me. They want to live peacefully, have families, and want to and live in love and light. But instead of living a life in peace, they have to duck and cover. And I pray for them, and I pray for peace for all.

Auctioning at a real estate auction. Ben Sr auctioning, Ben Jr. 'supervising'.

Waldo Wisdom #31

Impossible ideas don't limit us – they expand our opportunities.

The Difference Between Impossible and I'm Possible

As a businessman who's been around the block a time or two, I have a fondness for these words: "it can't be done." Generally when I hear that - I know I'm on to something big.

Case in point: in the mid-1970's, I decided to try a different way of selling real estate in the Gainesville area: real estate auctions. I'd just held a large real estate auction in another part of Florida that was highly successful and brought in more than the seller was anticipating. With that success under my belt, why not do it in Gainesville area?

When I began advertising the concept in the Gainesville newspapers and to area realtors, a respected Gainesville Realtor called me and said, "I see you going to try and sell real estate at auction, and I thought I'd tell you that it won't work in this part of the country. It may work in other parts, but it can't be done here. So, you're wasting your time. Just thought I'd let you know."

This realtor didn't know my mantra, "The only difference between impossible and I'm possible is an apostrophe!" He had no idea of all the impossible things I'd already done.

He didn't know that I'd grown up working hard for everything I got. We were poor, so my childhood away from school was spent picking watermelons, working the bean barn, working on a chicken farm, pumping gas, and doing various odd jobs. To get lunch at school, I cleaned the cafeteria! (There was no free lunch program in my day.)

He didn't know that I had already built a business that was supposed to be impossible. My auto auction in Albany was a highly successful enterprise that had taken my family to the next level. Before opening that business, a local car dealer told me that "six other people have tried to make an auto auction work here over the past six years, and all of them failed; I wish you well, but it can't be done."

The Realtor also didn't know that a few weeks before his "advice," that I had held a very successful real estate auction in Ponce Inlet, FL. Even though it was my FIRST real estate auction, I had put my heart and soul into making sure that I did everything in my power to do a great job for my client. After this auction, I knew I wanted to be of service to others by selling their real estate at auction. Sure, it was unconventional, but that would differentiate me from all the other real estate brokers.

When I started this new way of selling property in the Gainesville area, I knew this concept was looked at very cautiously by prospective sellers. Most were not use to the idea and slow to buy-in. To show the world just what the auction process would do, I bought a 200-acre farm, divided it up and auctioned it off. When all was said and done, I'd doubled my investment.

With this outcome, this auction process caught on. Over the last 30 years, I have sold thousands of properties amounting to tens of millions in sales doing something that a well-intentioned and seasoned real estate broker said wouldn't work.

So why do some people think or say it can't be done? Is it because in a very basic way, they fear change, the unknown? Could it be they fear trying something new and want to maintain the status quo? Or, maybe they have a fear that you might accomplish something they wish they had the gumption to try. I suggest you consider this: these impossible ideas don't limit us – they expand our opportunities if we open up to them!

My challenge to you is to think of those people who have done things that others said couldn't be done. Think of the Wright Brothers assembling their impossible aircraft in the back of a bicycle shop. Think of Henry Ford and his crazy goal of making affordable automobiles for the masses. Think of Steve Jobs combining a computer and the phone to make a device that might be in your hands right now.

You and YOU alone determine whether or not something can be done! I encourage you to go for it!

When someone tells you that "it can't be done," just remember that only an apostrophe is the difference between impossible and I'm possible!

Ben Jr. and Ben Sr.

Waldo Wisdom #32

Children learn from your actions.

The Cat's in the Cradle

In 1987, when my son, Ben, Jr., was 12 years old, I was concerned that he needed a structured after school activity. His mother and I had divorced, I was traveling a lot due to business opportunities, and I was concerned about what he might be doing after school until his mother came home from work. My quick solution to this problem was to convince him to play football at the Boy's Club.

Two years earlier, he had played Boy's Club football, but it had not been a good experience because of his coach. This coach was so bad; the Boys' Club dismissed him from coaching - and he was an unpaid volunteer! So, the next two years Ben, Jr. didn't want to play and I didn't press it.

But now, as he was getting older and more apt to go out and find inventive things to do after school, I started pressing him to sign up and play again. Every day for a week, I broached the idea, but I just wasn't having any success convincing him. As the deadline for registration approached, I implored him to sign up and play. "It'll be good for you! You are such a great athlete!"

Without hesitation, he looked up to me and said, "I'll play if you'll coach." WHAT did my son just say? .....WHAT did I just hear?

His comeback hit me like a ton of bricks. I'm a busy man! I am so busy that I have a pilot flying me throughout the southeast and as far away as Texas, West Virginia and Ohio. I have people to see, deals to make, money to earn! But all of a sudden, in the back of my mind, I heard Cat Stevens singing "the cat's in the cradle and the silver spoon" and "when you comin' home dad, I don't know when - but we'll get together then."

My son was reaching out. He wanted to spend time with me. (A lot of kids at that age don't even want to be seen with their parents). And Cat Stevens got a little louder in my head singing, "I'm gonna be like you, dad, you know I wanna be like you."

As I wrenched my heart out of my throat, I heard myself say, "Yes, l will coach."

Coaching changed my work and travel schedule drastically as I now had to be at the Boy's Club every day, ready for the players. But, looking back on it, it's one of the best parenting decisions I have ever made. Not only did I show Ben Jr. that I cared enough about him to invest my time to coach his team, but it also gave us quality time to share in something we had in common, the love of football. I went on to coach his team for the next few years until he was too old to play Boy's Club football.

I often wonder what would have happened if I'd have ignored his request. What if I'd have put money ahead of my children? Would he be who he is today? Would he have emulated me and put money before his children?

Today, Ben, Jr. has two children of his own, a boy and a girl, and coaches both in their respective sports. As I sit back and watch him with his kids, I again hear Cat Stevens singing, "I'm gonna be like you, dad, you know I wanna be like you." Knowing the wonderful father he is and the good example he is for Jacob and Kate to emulate makes me proud. Ben Jr. taught me a crucial lesson in Waldo Wisdom: Children learn from your actions.

If Ben, Jr's children are "gonna be like him," the positive legacy of one simple decision in 1987 will roll on into generations to come.

Ben with his daughter, Ashley.

Waldo Wisdom #33

School is never out.

Love and Respect

When my two children, Ashley and Ben, Jr., were young, one of the most important things I wanted for them was the ability to take care of themselves well. Ashley was eight and Ben Jr. was five when their mother and I divorced. Because they were now not with me on a daily basis, my focus shifted from a physical focal point to a conscious focal point. Accordingly, I took every opportunity to impart various lessons that I thought would be helpful throughout their lives. No doubt, experiencing my father's passing at 16 encouraged me to impart a little "Waldo Wisdom" to prepare them for whatever came their way.

When Ashley was in high school, she decided to live with me. We had not lived in the same house since she was 8, and this was a growing time for the both of us. As Ashley was learning about life and "becoming," I was learning how to be a single father and parent of a teenage daughter. Yes, there were a few sleepless nights. I wanted to protect her from harm, yet I knew that I had to give her the latitude to become who she wanted to become.

As the days and months went by, I marveled at her evolution. She was savvy and had a knack for figuring out how to do things. And, she was logical and determined to accomplish her goals. For example, on the night of her senior prom, she was out beyond curfew. I was very strict with her curfew and was growing more anxious as every minute passed. When the phone rang, I picked it up expecting to impart a few choice words of wisdom and she calmly said, "First, I want you to know that I'm OK. Next, I know I'm supposed to be home right now, but I want to enjoy prom night longer and have fun with my friends, so I've decided to do that. Don't worry about me; I'll be fine. And, I accept any consequences you deem fit for my actions." My first thought was, "How dare you to defy my rule?" Thinking about it more, I was impressed that she was taking charge of her 'becoming' and that she accepted responsibility for her actions. Her 'becoming' challenged me and made me come to 'grips' that she was a senior in high school and would soon be out in the world on her own!

Shortly after her prom came her graduation from high school. My little girl was no longer a little girl and was getting ready to attend college. She decided to go to Georgia Southern University in Statesboro, GA, some 200 miles from home. Her decision brought on some consternation as she would be SO far from home and away from my oversight. I was concerned that my 'little girl' might succumb to peer pressure and make some choices that she might regret. Deep down inside I knew I needed to accept the fact that Ashley was growing up and that if I truly wanted her to 'become' who she wanted to become, I needed to release control and, indeed, support her evolution. It was just so hard to give up control because I wanted to ensure that she was safe and happy!

Little did I know that on our trip to get her moved in at Georgia Southern, her actions would ease my fears about her safety and welfare.

After Ashley had finished packing her car, I loaded it on a car dolly that I had hitched onto my 40' Blue Bird Motor Coach. The route I decided to travel was U.S. Hwy. 301, which is the road my parents drove when we traveled from Waldo to their hometown in North Carolina.

Due to Interstate I-95 being built somewhat parallel to it, U.S. Hwy 301 was still a two-lane road, with narrow bridges that had concrete sidewalls. In the early afternoon, I became sleepy and told Ashley, "I know you are anxious to get to Statesboro, but I need to pull over and take a nap." To that, Ashley said, "Dad, I can drive." "But you've never driven this or anything like this," I said with quite a bit of anxiety in my voice. "Driving this is different than driving a car." To that, she replied with sincere confidence, "Just tell me how and I'll do it." Since there was very little traffic on the road, I decided I would let her drive.

I pulled the motor coach over and then explained, "This vehicle is wider than a normal car and in driving it, there's a sensation that you're not driving in the middle of your driving lane as you'll think that you are indeed driving somewhat in the oncoming traffic's lane. Thus, you will have a tendency to drive on the very right side of the lane, and you may go off the road onto the shoulder." So, after her assurance that she understood, I let her take the wheel. I said to myself, "I better sit in the passenger's seat for a bit just to make sure she can drive this thing." I no more than had that thought, when I saw one of those very narrow bridges with concrete sidewalls just a short distance ahead. It caused me some concern but, I thought Ashley would drive down the middle of the bridge and thus stay away from the concrete wall, which is what I would have done. This thought was short lived when I saw a huge log truck, loaded down with logs, coming towards us and would enter the bridge at the same time we would!

My first inclination was to shout out instructions on how to keep the Motor Coach centered in 'our' lane so she would not hit the sidewall or the oncoming truck!! But quickly, I decided to trust her enough to implement the instructions I had given her and not to say something that might cause her to question herself. I must say, it was a good decision. Ashley didn't panic and coolly kept the motor coach in her lane. Within the first two minutes of operating the motorcoach, she passed the ultimate driving challenge with flying colors!!

In looking back on that incident, I realize that it taught me a valuable lesson. Once you've explained something, get out of that person's way and trust them to accomplish the task. Show them that respect. Hovering over and critiquing them may cause feelings of insecurity and the outcome may very well be quite inferior to what you had initially desired. Love and respect trumps insecurity and distrust every time.

My interactions with Ashley over the subsequent years have been significantly influenced by this revelation. Our discussions on life's challenges now flow through channels of love and respect. Has she always done everything in her life as I would have done? No. And thank God for that - because her accomplishments and her mistakes (I like to call them 'learning experiences') have shaped her into the wonderful woman she has become!

Now that Ashley has children of her own, I watch their interactions, and I see her moving through challenges and learning opportunities with Maddy and Carson with the same love and respect that she and I have for each other to this day. I see Maddy and Carson positively evolving, and I know they will continue to grow with a loving and respectful spirit! I am awed at the person my wonderful daughter, Ashley, has 'become.'

One of my favorite pieces of Waldo Wisdom is that school is never out. This country boy is never too old or too proud to learn from his daughter. Thank you, Ashley, for teaching me about love and respect.

Ben (right) with his friend John Schroepfer (left).

Waldo Wisdom #34

There is power in forgiveness.

Forgiveness

Back in the 70's, I decided to purchase some shares of stock of a local bank that was expanding. Because of the number I bought, I was elected to serve on the Board of Directors. It was quite interesting; me being in my mid 20's and young enough to be the son of any of the other Board members. As a new member, I initially did what I was brought up to do, and that was to listen, especially to those who are older who had more experience.

As the years went by and my confidence increased, I began to express opinions on various issues, including potential loans that needed Board approval. There was this one particular loan that the Bank Board Chairman and I had differing opinions. We had been quite friendly before this incident, but the unpleasantness of the disagreement led to the demise of our friendship. Unfortunately, this contention became an issue, and when election time came around, he was not reelected to the Board.

Some years later, a good friend, John Schroepfer (Schroe), asked me if I would be interested in joining the Rotary Club of Gainesville. With close to 300 members, this club was the largest Rotary Club in Gainesville and a great place to make contacts. I accepted his invitation and completed my application of which Schroe submitted to the Rotary Board.

A few weeks later, I found out that one Rotarian objected to my application. I found this to be quite puzzling as I felt I was a respected member of the community! Who in the world would have a problem with my membership in a service club?! Of course, it turned out to be the former Bank Board Chairman (BBC).

I explained to Schroe what happened between the BBC and myself and that the issue was of management styles and not of any wrongdoing on anyone's part. He passed this information along to the Rotary Board, who accepted my explanation and approved my application for membership.

As the years passed, I would occasionally see the BBC at Rotary meetings, and we would just pass each other by with no acknowledgment of the other's existence. I figured I'd just ignore him and thus, wouldn't have to deal with him.

Then in January of 2000, my friend Schroe came to me with an interesting proposition. "There's a group of us going to Honduras to rebuild houses for hurricane victims, and we have an opening," said Schroe. "Your building skills would be such a valuable asset to the project, and I'd love for you to go with us."

Schroe then told me about the hardships facing the Hondurans as they tried to rebuild after Hurricane Mitch. This hurricane struck Central America, leaving more than 11,000 people dead, destroying hundreds of thousands of homes and causing more than $5 billion in damages. At the time, it was reported to be the deadliest hurricane to hit the Western Hemisphere in more than 200 years.

Even though I hadn't made a trip like this before, after hearing Schroe outline the journey, deep down I knew I wanted to go. So I signed up.

A few weeks later, our team of volunteers met to load our gear into a van and head to the airport. And guess who was in the van?! BBC!

Wow! How was this going to play out? We hadn't spoken in more than 20 years!

At first, I was uncomfortable about this development. Did I really want to spend two weeks with a man whom I wasn't speaking? But just as quickly, I banished that thought from my mind and decided 20 years was long enough not to at least say a 'hello' to someone. So, I swallowed my pride and extended a hand. We shook hands, said a lackluster "good morning" and that was that.

At the worksite in Honduras, I often found BBC and myself working in the same proximity, sometimes literally side by side. As the days went on, I saw firsthand how hard he was working even though he was much older than everyone else on the trip. I thought to myself, "A man who helps others with this kind of effort and care is someone I want as a friend." At that moment, I let go of the past, pushed down my ego, opened my heart, and showed him love and respect.

And wonder upon wonders; he reciprocated. I would take him a bottle of water, and he would enthusiastically thank me. He accepted my efforts to reach out and over the remainder of the mission trip, he extended acts of kindness to me as well.

When we returned from Honduras, the friendship continued. When we worked on other projects together or saw each other at Rotary or other events, we always met with a hearty handshake and a very warm greeting - often embracing. And, this friendship was better and deeper than the one we'd had years before. Not too many years later, BBC passed away. I had the honor to serve as the chaplain at his funeral which touched me greatly. As I participated in his funeral service, I felt so grateful for our mission trip, knowing that it helped us make amends and become friends again before it was too late.

Waldo Wisdom has taught me that there is a power in forgiveness. Think about it this way – before the Honduras trip; I'd walk into Rotary and feel angst if BBC and I were in the same vicinity. Once we became friends again, I had the freedom to walk into my Rotary Club and be in complete peace and happy to see him. This quote by Lewis B. Smedes says it all, "To forgive is to set the prisoner free, and realize the prisoner was you."

Ashley during her modeling career.

Waldo Wisdom #35

Ask for what you want, otherwise,
you will get what others want to give you.

Knock and the Door Will Open

In 1994, my daughter, Ashley, graduated from college
with a degree in child psychology. Upon graduation she
began counseling middle school children, doing her best to
help them improve their life. While it was mentally and
emotionally rewarding, the financial benefits were not -
and she found herself in the unenviable position of having
to borrow money to have a reasonable lifestyle. While I was
happy to help her out, after a couple of years, I was
concerned that she was on a dead-end road.

I told her that the reason that I was in a position to help
her financially was that I had worked hard, had made some
good business decisions and that now these ventures were
paying off. But, to continue to be profitable, these
enterprises were dependent upon my involvement on a
day-to-day basis. If I weren't around, for whatever reason,
the flow of funds would dry up. I implored her to either go
back to college and get a doctorate or consider coming to
work for my company and learn the business.

In 1996, Ashley started working for me. She was doing a
good job, but after a while, I could tell her heart wasn't in

it. After a father-daughter heart-to-heart talk, she agreed that she wasn't happy working for Campen Enterprises.

As her father, and biggest fan, I wanted her to be happy. I know that when you do what you love, you never work a day in your life. So I asked her, "WHAT is it that you REALLY want to do? What is your passion in life?"

Without hesitation, she said, "I want to be a mom." I could tell that she was truly speaking from her heart. And I excitedly responded, "That's wonderful! I think you should be! You'd make a great mom!"

She quickly reminded me that she wasn't married, and didn't even have a boyfriend.

"What want is to be married to someone I love, have children and raise them in a family environment," I told her I respected her goals and that she should keep her sights, her energy, and her thoughts fixed on that dream becoming a reality.

Since having a family wasn't something she would start immediately, I asked, "In the meantime, what else really interests you?"

"I would like to go into modeling," she said. And that - she did. To be more readily available to her agency for modeling jobs, she decided to move to Miami. Although this was an exciting time for her, I could always tell that having a family was in the forefront of her thoughts.

Then, in March of 2000, Ashley drove up to Gainesville to attend the annual Rotary Wild Game Feast. "Ashley," I said, "you are looking quite spiffy if I might say so!" She replied with a bubbly smile, "Yes, I know. I'm going to meet my husband tonight, so I thought I'd dress accordingly!" I just smiled loving her enthusiasm and optimism.

As the evening unfolded, she met a handsome young man named Andy. And, they were completely taken with each other. After 18 months of courtship, he asked me for her hand in marriage.

Today, they are the parents of a daughter, Maddy, and a son, Carson, both of whom I love very much. And, Ashley is a fantastic mom. Yes, I know, your mom/wife/daughter are wonderful moms - but my daughter is just amazing. Her patience, her wisdom, and her ability to turn potentially bad situations into good situations are all astounding. When I am with her and her family, I can see an aura of love and happiness surrounding her. It's pure joy.

Waldo Wisdom tells us that if you don't ask for what you want, you will only get what others want to give you.

When you ask for what you want and hold that thought in your mind, you set in motion the manifestation process. Asking is like opening the door to an airless chamber. Once you open this door, all of the air will naturally come rushing in.

"Ask, and it will be given to you; seek, and you will find; knock, and it will be opened to you. - Matthew 7:7."

Ben Campen and Bhichai Rattakul in Phuket, Thailand soon after the 2004 Southeast Asia Tsunami.

Waldo Wisdom #36

We GAIN abundance through GIVING.

Doing Good in the World

As a child, my mother modeled the giving soul. Of course, she gave to her family; but she gave to others, too. Even when we didn't have much, she volunteered and gave what she could - and it was always meaningful. Her example is part of my soul, and why I am compelled to do what I can when people are in need.

On January 3, 2005, I had just returned home from my sister's house in Georgia where my mother and I had celebrated Christmas. It was such a wonderful holiday, and we had so much fun visiting with each other, that we hadn't watched TV in days.

When I returned home to Gainesville, I turned on the television and saw the horror that was happening in Southeast Asia. A week before, there had been a devastating tsunami and the estimates were that more than 150,000 people had lost their lives.

As I watched the news reports, I also learned that there were thousands of injured people and that thousands upon thousands had lost their homes. A report that touched my heart was the story of a teenager who had been aboard a train washed off the tracks by the tsunami. This young man survived, but 1,500 people on that train had perished. He was so grateful that he had survived but mourned the loss of so many.

After watching the news reports, my heart told me to go to Southeast Asia and see if I could help the surviving victims. Having been on mission trips to Central America with other Rotarians, I reached out to the members of my Rotary Club. The next morning, I received a call from a fellow Rotarian who was the Executive Director of the Alachua County Medical Society. She informed me that two doctors and two nurses wanted to go to Southeast Asia and that one of them had a physician friend in Bangkok who would work as our local contact. By the end of the week, we were airborne and on our way to Thailand. My role was to be of assistance to the doctors and nurses.

Once we arrived in southern Thailand, we went to various refugee camps. The doctors and nurses went to the medical tents to do what they could, while I visited with some of the refugees in the camps.

I had brought cash with me, some donated by family and friends as well as members of my Rotary Club, and I walked around the camp seeking out mothers who had babies in their arms to give them a $10 bill. I find that my giving funds directly to an individual in need is a very meaningful way, if not the most meaningful way, to help. I then would know exactly to whom the money went. And, a $10 bill given to a tsunami victim in Thailand would go a long way as that was equivalent to many days wages - and when they bought needed goods from local merchants, it would help stimulate the local economy, helping even more who had suffered the fallout of the terrible tsunami. Waldo

Wisdom says that giving in meaningful ways helps the receiver and inspires the giver. Seeing the faces of those mothers and their children as I handed them $10 bills inspired me to do more.

As the days progressed and the medical needs lessened, the team planned their return home. But, I felt that I hadn't done enough. So, as the doctors and nurses headed to the airport to fly back to Gainesville, I went to the hard-hit area of Phuket.

Since I am a Rotarian, I went to a Rotary meeting in Phuket, where I hoped to find some direction. As luck would have it, I met Chaisinn Manninan, the Chairman of all the Rotary Clubs in Thailand. He, in turn, introduced me to Bhichai Rattakul, Past President of Rotary International and former Deputy Prime Minister of Thailand. Bhichai had flown down from his home in Bangkok that very same day and was there to take the Rotary Chairman and District Governors to the affected areas to make initial plans for Rotary's part in the recovery and rebuilding process. After a brief visit with Bhichai, we found in each other to be kindred spirits. He invited me to travel to the affected areas with him, Chaisinn and Chaisinn's wife, Prarom.

Even though Bhichai is older than me, he had the vitality of a young man. His dedication to service and his desire to help tsunami victims in a meaningful way was infectious to all around him. I knew that I had come to the right place at the right time and met the right person! As he formed and explained his ideas and Rotary's plans, I began to see where I could help.

During my final hours in Thailand, Bhichai strongly suggested that I go to Sri Lanka, a country that had also been hit hard by the tsunami. His suggestion intrigued me, and I said 'yes' to it and the next morning Bhichai made phone calls to some of his Rotary friends in Sri Lanka to arrange logistics.

The next morning I was touring the affected coastline, stopping along the way to give $10 bills to displaced people who had lost their homes and were lined up beside the roadway, looking to anyone for help.

Early afternoon, as we were making our way down to the southern tip of Sri Lanka, we came around a sharp curve, and there it was! The train I had seen on the news that had inspired me to make this journey of halfway around the world!! The hair stood up on the back of my neck as I had come full circle. In an act of defiance to the tsunami and their resolve to move forward, the local people had righted the fallen train back onto the tracks. It was a symbol of their courage and their dedication to rebuilding their lives.

Before returning to Gainesville, I told Bhichai that my plan was to go back to the U.S. to do presentations at Rotary Clubs and to other groups to give them a firsthand account of the devastation and inform them of Rotary's plan to build houses for those displaced by the tsunami. My goal was to raise funds to support the Rotary Clubs of Thailand in their efforts to build some 200 homes for tsunami victims. Furthermore, I told Bhichai that I wanted to return, with my son and son-in-law and others to physically participate in the building of those homes.

Over the following months, we raised more than $120,000 and in May of 2005, our local team consisting of five flew to southern Thailand to help with the home-building effort.

I feel fortunate to be a member Rotary! I had a passion for helping, and at every turn, Rotary was there to guide me to a path where I could be most effective - where my efforts would have the most meaning.

How frustrating would it have been for me if I'd have gone and not been able to do something I believed to be meaningful?

Doing something meaningful and being helpful to others is a core value I believe that most of us have. Sometimes we are at a loss as to just how to best make that happen. What can appear on the surface to be helpful may not be best.

This lesson hit home with me when I saw a news story called "When disaster relief brings anything but relief." The story revealed that when disaster strikes, people in the U.S. want to help. But, sometimes, individuals with the best of intentions can do more harm than good.

One example in this news report detailed the issues of donated bottled water to areas that are a great distance away. It's expensive to transport, difficult to store, and it requires a huge workforce to distribute. The article shows a picture of a warehouse storing bottled water and points out, "This water, it's about 100,000 liters, will provide drinking water for 40,000 people for one day. This amount of water to send from the United States, say, to West Africa -- and people did this -- costs about $300,000. But relief organizations with portable water purification units can produce the same amount, a 100,000 liters of water, for about $300."

Indeed, after the 2004 Indian Ocean tsunami, well-meaning people cleaned out their closets and sent bales of clothing to Indonesia on container ships. Included in these bales were winter coats, high heeled shoes, Halloween costumes, and other un-useful items. Because there was no time for disaster workers to sort and clean old clothes, the bales were opened and left on a beach for tsunami survivors to pick through. Unfortunately, this vast quantity of un-useful items became toxic and had to be destroyed. Local authorities burned it and let the tide carry it to sea.

Aid workers, unfortunately, see this quite often. They call it the "second disaster."

While in the refugee camps, I was delighted to see Shelter Boxes. The shelter box program was started by a Rotarian and helps more than 35,000 families each year. These boxes contain items needed for survival: a tent, water purification system, solar lighting, essential tools and cooking supplies. I was proud to see these tents with the Rotary logo on them in several camps in the areas I visited.

In a way, this may seem like a plug for Rotary, and that is because Rotary is the organization that I believe in and support. And, because there are Rotary Clubs all over the world, they are often one of the first groups on the scene and can tell you what is needed in an area affected by a disaster. I feel fortunate to belong to a group that makes meaningful contributions during difficult times.

I am confident that many who will read this are very generous people. I want to thank you for all the meaningful work you do for others and the financial support you give to very worthwhile endeavors. I know you don't do it for the thanks. You do it because you have a great heart that wants to do good for people in need. You inspire me.

My hope is that this writing inspires you as well to stay the course; to keep doing meaningful, positive and loving work to make the world a better place right in your community or even half way around the world.

Top Row: Andy, Maddy, Ashley, Ben Jr., Robin

Bottom Row: Carson, PaB, Kate, Jacob

Waldo Wisdom #37

At the end of your life, the amount in your bank account won't matter.

Resolving to Make Deposits

It was June 2011; I was in Austin, TX to locate a tract of land and conduct due diligence in the development of a new market similar to the ones I own in Asheville, NC, and Macon, GA. After locating a property, I spent considerable time and money meeting with government officials as well as professional engineers, doing my best to ascertain the viability of the project.

Additionally, I had spent considerable time lining up the additional funds needed to make this project work financially. Everything had the appearance of "GO, " and I was quite excited about the potential of such an opportunity in one of the fastest growing areas in the United States!

With only a few days away from closing on the purchase, something told me to fly to Jacksonville and have dinner with my son, Ben Jr., his wife, Robin, and their two children, Jacob (5) and Kate (3). I wanted to go over the new venture with Ben Jr. (which I easily could have done over the phone) but flying there would also give me a chance to visit and enjoy family time.

So, fly to JAX, I did. After meeting with Ben Jr. about the project, we made our way over to his house for dinner. As I played with Jacob and Kate, Ben Jr. and Robin cooked an excellent meal. Once dinner was over, Ben Jr. and Robin got up and began clearing off the table. Within moments, Jacob and Kate ran to me and climbed into my lap. They each put their arms around my neck and kissed me on the cheek and said "We've missed you so much. I love you, Pa B!" At that heart-piercing moment, something hit me. Their actions were unsolicited and not orchestrated. I thought, "What just happened in the core of my being?"

That night I couldn't sleep. My mind was buzzing – could I be seriously thinking about canceling this project because of a simple act of love from my grandchildren? I was about to make a substantial financial investment into a big time project that was going to consume an enormous amount of my time over the next few years. And, in doing so, I would miss spending time with not only Jacob and Kate but also my other grandchildren Maddy and Carson, my aging and wonderful mother, not to mention spending time with my daughter, Ashley and her husband, Andy, in addition to Ben and Robin.

I am very close to my family. And, to think, I was just about to embark on a project over 1,000 miles away! Sleeping that night was not to be as I just kept thinking and feeling that this project wasn't really what I wanted in my life.....that what I wanted was time to spend with my family and being present and to share in their lives, be it my grandchildren, children or my mother. By dawn, I was resolved.

I made a resolution to put family first. That day, I flew back to Austin and canceled the project.

I have made some critical decisions in my life, but I can't think of any one decision that was more monumental than this one; to change direction 180 degrees. Even though the business opportunity was fantastic, it could not ever be as meaningful as time with my family! Family time is something that no amount of money can buy. I know that I made the right decision.

Today, think about the things that take time away from family. If you work a lot, you may want to consider the impact on your family. Yes, to work hard and be determined to be successful is admirable. Yes, doing our very best is important. However, there is a balance to life. I encourage you to enjoy your family as much as you can! Today could be the day that you influence your child or grandchild to excel. Today could be the day that you give a piece of advice that could change their world for the better. Today could be the day you show them how important they are – influencing them to show this kind of love to their children as well as to others. Think of your time with family as a deposit and investment into their future well-being.

Who knows when our last day on earth will be? Waldo Wisdom reminds us that at the end of your life, the amount of money in your bank account won't matter; it's the deposits made in the lives of your family. The time you spent with your family and the love you shared with them will resonate not only in their being but for generations to come. To me, that means everything.

Ben Jr. and Ben Sr.

Waldo Wisdom #38

You gain independence when you empower others.

Relinquishing the Reins

When I went into business for myself at the age of 22, I made myself "the decider." I did the hiring and the firing. I set the hours. I made the decisions as to what properties my companies would buy, how they would operate when they were sold and what the asking price would be. Initially, I even determined the little things like where we would purchase office supplies. I was the COO as well as President, CEO and the CFO. I was indeed hands-on and very involved on the front lines and back lines equally. Micromanaging comes naturally to me as I was raised to be responsible for what happens in my life. Needless to say, this took an enormous amount of energy, but it was, to me, just something that goes along with owning a business.

It took several years before I could empower a small number of top employees to purchase small ticket items. But the decisions about investments and improvements as well as determining what assets we would sell would continue to be made by me.

I'm certain that a considerable amount of this 'control' thought process was because I wanted to do my very best to ensure my businesses would be successful. Having grown up in an economically challenged family, I didn't want to squander the opportunities that were before me.

Early in my career, my son, Ben, Jr. took a lot of interest in my businesses. From age 5, he would go with me to help measure out buildings and parcels of land that I was preparing to sell. During summer breaks in school (both high school and college), Ben, Jr. would do many various things for me including measuring the property, erecting signs and building huge billboards from plans I provided, all on his own. And, he took a great deal of pride in his workmanship; he did it all very well.

During those years, as he was growing up, many friends who knew my son, would say things like, "I bet you are grooming him to take over your businesses one day." I promptly replied, "Actually, I'm not. I want him to pursue and do what he wants to. That's going to be his choice." Even though I was hoping he would, I just wanted it to be HIS decision.

When he graduated from college, he asked if he could work for my company. Of course, I was elated! I first had him work on only the small projects. As time went on, I knew that the only way for him to grow was to learn by doing.

So, as I slowly relinquished control of projects and business decisions, I saw Ben, Jr. take full responsibility for projects that he oversaw. From drawing out the plans to hiring necessary personnel and contractors and suppliers, he did, and still does today, a fantastic job!

For the most part, he conducted business just like I had. But, sometimes he took a different tack which caused me a little angst. Standing back and watching was somewhat difficult at times, because, there again, I had been THE decision-maker for over 30 years!

A few years later, Ben Jr. called me about a new project. We had a large piece of unproductive land on the books, and there was new development was happening nearby. His idea was to build a subdivision on this property. And he didn't exactly ask me if he could do it. This conversation was more of a discussion peer to peer.

So he built the subdivision with absolutely no help from me. He negotiated everything with the city and county, did all the permitting, marketed the development and finally sold the lots while I sat back and watched. And, he made the company a pretty penny.

A few months later, as I was reading my emails, I read one from him, and I noticed that he had changed his title from 'Vice-President' to 'President' of Ben Campen Companies. Wow!! I couldn't help but grin from ear to ear. Without even a hint of him taking on the title, he just did it! He assumed the lead in our company!

While it made me very proud of my son, it was a whole new experience for me. The realization that he assumed the reins and now it was in full play.   But, the funny thing was - I wasn't concerned. His history of good business decisions, clear thinking, and innovation, had sold me. Besides, he had to be good, of course, because I trained him!

Handing over the reins is quite empowering to both you and the recipient of the reins. Whether it is letting your grown children host Thanksgiving dinner, allowing your employees to handle more of your company, or handing over your life's work to your children - the idea of giving up something that has been a part of your life can give you pause. But trust me, you aren't giving anything up. You are helping the next generation gain knowledge and experience under your watchful eye.

Waldo Wisdom says that you gain independence when you empower others. It also frees you up to sleep late on Thanksgiving mornings, gives you the freedom to work on different projects, and time to do good in the community and the world.

Maddy, Kate, PaB, Carson and Jacob

Waldo Wisdom #39

Anytime is the right time to empower a child.

The Best Present

I love being with my family at Christmastime. To help keep the stress out of Christmas, a couple of years ago, the adults decided to do a Secret Santa gift exchange. We put the names of the adults into a hat; everyone pulls out a name, and then they buy a present for that person. The gifts can be no more than $50, and it wrapped in newspaper that has the letters of the recipient circled in the newsprint. This gift exchange is so much fun and only buying one gift helps to lessen holiday stress.

But, Secret Santa is for the adults only, and I still had to figure out what to buy for my four grandchildren. And who knows what they are into from year to year? And, I wanted to be sure to spend the same amount on each of them. At any rate, it was going to be challenging to get something for each of them that they would enjoy and yet be a meaningful gift.

So, after conferring with my children, it was suggested that I give them the universal catch-all gift: money. But, cash seemed too impersonal, so I thought I'd add some fun time with PaB (that's me). I decided to give each of them $50 along with this invitation:

An Invitation

To: Maddox, Jacob, Carson & Kate
From: Pa B
Date: December 26th
Time: Pa B will pick you up at your house:
- *Jacob & Kate at 2 pm and*
- *Maddy & Carson at 2:15*

You are invited to a day with PaB
- *Pa B will give you $50 that you may spend however you like. You may spend it during our day, or not.*
- *Each gets 30 minutes shopping at the store of your choice.*
- *We all go out for pizza at your favorite pizza place.*
- *Then we all go to a movie of your choosing*
- *After the movie, we all go for ice cream.*

    The first year I did this, I was somewhat anxious as to how they would respond. When all I heard was a polite "thank-you," it seemed like their enthusiasm was a little cool. This response made me anxious about the outing, and I was concerned that I'd given them the wrong gift.

    But the next day, they had such a great time that my fears were unfounded. I gave them free reign to purchase whatever they wanted with their money or to save part or all of it, and I let them make all their own decisions. It was interesting to watch each of them consider how to spend their money. As they were picking out items, I had each of them add up their items and also to figure out the tax to arrive at the total cost of their selections. More than once, I was asked if I would cover a small overage to which I informed them that I would not. Then I watched them make the decision as to what they would put back and what they would make a priority and ultimately buy. Indeed, I could sense the personal empowerment in each of them that took place as they made their own choices without any adult interference or direction. They had a wonderful time! After shopping, we ate at the pizza parlor, went to the movie and then went to the ice cream store. When I dropped them at home, the hugs and the smiles they gave me let me know that this outing truly was the perfect gift!

I was so pleased with the whole outing that the following year, I gave them the same gift. On Christmas Day, as I passed out the envelopes to each at the same time, my youngest granddaughter yelled out, "Yeah!! I know what it is; it's the BEST present in the whole wide world!!" To which, the three other grandchildren yelled out a BIG "Yeah!! It IS!" As they tore into their envelopes, my heart overflowed with joy and tears filled my eyes as I saw their happiness about the future outing with PaB.

It was interesting for me to realize that my grandchildren could teach me a lesson in Waldo Wisdom. But they showed me that anytime is the right time to empower a child. On this simple outing, they made their own decisions within the outlined parameters. And they were so appreciative that I did not interfere with their decision-making process. I was just looking for the right Christmas present and didn't realize how right it was until

I saw how this simple act changed the way they thought about their choices and the enormous amount of fun we five had together on the entire outing

Guess what PaB will be giving his four grandchildren for Christmas this year?!!! Until they get tired of going on the outing with me, I'll be giving them this gift every year!

Made in the USA
Charleston, SC
26 February 2017